W H Y
NORMA
JEAN
KILLED
MARILYN
MONROE

D1211491

3 1705 00214 3227

W H Y
NORMA
J E A N
KILLED
MARILYN
MONROE

STATE LIBRARY OF OHIO
SEO Regional Library
Caldwell, Ohio 43724

Books by Lucy Freeman

ON PSYCHOLOGY AND PSYCHOANALYSIS
Fight Against Fears, Crown 1952
The Beloved Prison, A Journey Into the Unknown Self, St. Martin's Press 1989
Our Wish To Kill: The Murder in All Our Hearts (with Dr Herbert S. Stean),
    St. Martin's Press 1991, Avon Paperback 1992

BIOGRAPHY
Remember Me to Tom, G. P. Putnam's Sons, 1963
Reflections of a Pioneer Psychiatrist (with Dr. Karl Menninger), Thomas Y. Crowell, 1953
America's First Feminist: Deborah Sampson, The Woman Who Fought in the
    Revolutionary War as a Man, Paragon Press, 1992

BASED ON FACT
Betrayal, Stein and Day, 1976 (TV Movie)
Before I Kill More, Crown, 1955
Psychologist With Gun (with Dr. Harvey Schlossberg),
    Coward, McCann and Geoghegan, 1974 (TV Series)

Published by GLOBAL RIGHTS LTD., 540 West Aldine, Chicago, IL 60057
Distributed through Login Brothers Book Company,
    1436 West Randolph Street, Chicago,IL 60607

First Printing, June 1992
10 9 8 7 6 5 4 3 2 1
Copyright © 1992 by Lucy Freeman and Eddie Jaffe
All rights reserved.

LIBRARY OF CONGRESS CATALOGING-IN-PUBLICATION DATA
Freeman, Lucy/Jaffe, Eddie
        Why Norma Jean Killed Marilyn Monroe / Lucy Freeman
           ISBN 1-880141-13-2

Printed in the United States of America

Cover Jacket Photograph © 1957 by Sam Shaw
    Used by permission of the Shaw Family Collection

Design of this entire publication © 1992 by Bob Essman

Without limiting the rights under copyrights reserved above, no part of this
publication may be reproduced, stored in or introduced into a retrieval system,
or transmitted, in any form, or by any means (electronic, mechanical,
photocopying, recording or otherwise), without the prior written permission of
both the copyright owners and the above publisher of this book.

This book is dedicated
to those in whom
the terror of childhood has
created suicidal feelings
with the hope that
Marilyn Monroe's tragic story
may help them understand themselves
more deeply and find new peace.

Lucy Freeman

•

My Contribution to this book was
inspired by the memories of
Jim Henaghan and Sidney Skolsky
of the Hollywood press,
two of Marilyn's closest advisors.
They enabled her to survive the forces
against her in Hollywood and
taught me to understand
what a remarkable woman she was.

Eddie Jaffe

Norma Jean the infant
© Robert F. Slatzer

CONTENTS

**Dr. Ralph Greenson, who tried to
save Marilyn**

ACKNOWLEDGMENTS

Eddie Jaffe, who spent most of his life involved with the motion picture industry on an international basis but especially in Hollywood, came to me three years ago with the idea of a "new" book on Marilyn Monroe.

"So many books have been written about her there's nothing new," I said.

"Yes, there is," he pointed out. "Why don't you, an expert in the field of the human mind and a past president of the Mystery Writers of America, write about the hidden reasons Marilyn committed suicide?"

I confessed, "I've only read a few of the eighty-five books about her, two by my friend Fred Lawrence Guiles, who wrote *Norma Jean* and *Legend: The Life and Death of Marilyn Monroe*. But I could read more and find out if anyone told of the real and unreal reasons she killed herself."

Eddie and I first met when I was a reporter on *The New York Times* and we were both seeing psychoanalysts. He was a fan of analysts the way other men were of sports heroes. I wouldn't have been surprised if he met the ocean liners bringing in from Europe such psychoanalysts as Dr. Theodor Reik, Dr. Carl Fulton Sulzberger and Dr. Fredrick Hacker who founded the clinic named after him in Los Angeles. The first day Dr. Hacker spent in America he walked in Central Park with another analyst Eddie knew, who introduced him to Dr. Hacker. Eddie said, "H'ya, Doc." Dr. Hacker turned to the other analyst, said, "I was concerned about my future in America but after a warm greeting like 'H'ya, Doc?' I'm no longer worried."

Mrs. Hildi Greenson, wife of the late Dr. Ralph Greenson, Marilyn's psychoanalyst in Los Angeles during the star's last year, graciously invited me into her home and answered many questions. She recalled Marilyn's daily visits to her house as a patient and the countless times she stayed as a guest in the evenings with the whole family present. When I thanked Mrs. Greenson for her contributions to this book, she wrote, "Your psychoanalytic insight gives a new dimension not found in other books, in addition to a fuller picture of Marilyn."

Mrs. Greenson's daughter, Joan Greenson Aebi, also provided new information about her relationship to Marilyn, as she tried to help the troubled movie icon feel welcome in the house that provided her not only with psychoanalytic awareness about her past life but also enabled her to participate in the closeness of family life.

Paul Moor, author and journalist, a friend of Dr. Greenson, also gave important clues and the late Dr. Martin Grotjahn, professor emeritus at the University of California at Los Angeles, psychoanalyst for a number of Hollywood stars, contributed valuable thoughts.

I also thank Fred Guiles, who provided additional information not mentioned in his two books. Felice Ingersoll, who knew Marilyn at the start of both their careers when they appeared in 1948 in *Scudda Hoo! Scudda Hay!*, William Stadium, who wrote *Marilyn Monroe Confidential* with Lena Pepitone, and Sam Shaw, photographer and movie producer, who also wrote *The Joy of Marilyn in the Camera Eye*, gave Eddie much valuable information.

When I had asked Eddie what he thought of my writing *Fight Against Fear*, describing my psychoanalysis, he said, "Worst idea I ever heard of for a book." He did not apologize until many years later after the book sold one million copies worldwide. Now he said, "If a million people were interested in *your* analysis, how many more would want to know what happened in Marilyn's therapy?"

Thus this book, describing why Marilyn killed herself after four years of therapy with Dr. Marianne Kris, then a year with Dr. Ralph Greenson, both well-known psychoanalysts.

My deepest thanks to Eddie, co-author of this book, for his help all along the way as we both searched for a true understanding of why Norma Jean felt so desperate she obliterated Marilyn Monroe from the face of the earth, though she has never disappeared as far as her fans are concerned.

I am also grateful to Denis McKeown for his excellent copy editing and helpful contributions, Bob Essman, designer of the jacket and the book, and Howard Cohen, of HSC Communications.

Lucy Freeman
February, 1992

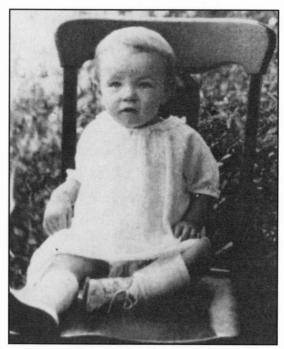

Norma Jean the toddler

© Robert F. Slatzer

1.
The Cry
For Help

It was a most unusual twosome. The Sex Goddess of Hollywood films and one of the world's most famous psychoanalysts.

Her mission was to try to face the unhappiness within her buried self. His mission was to try to save her very life, in danger of being abruptly ended by a strong wish to die.

Marilyn Monroe met Dr. Ralph Greenson for the first time in Bungalow 21 of the Beverly Hills Hotel in Los Angeles where she was staying as she filmed *Let's Make Love* in early 1960. Her psychoanalyst in New York, Dr. Marianne Kris, had called Dr. Greenson to ask if he would see her patient for a few sessions to help her over a difficult situation.

Dr. Kris explained that Marilyn was suffering "severe anxiety stress." She advised Dr. Greenson that Marilyn's incessant drinking of vodka and champagne, plus her endless doses of pills, were slowly driving her into death's outstretched arms. Marilyn had already attempted suicide a number of times but always been rescued at the last moment.

At this point Marilyn had taken the title of *Let's Make Love* literally— she had become sexually intimate with her leading man, French film legend Yves Montand. Long married to the equally acclaimed film actress Simone Signoret, Montand then suddenly called off all love-making with Marilyn, explaining he would never desert his French wife. America's Sex Goddess was once again abandoned.

After that first meeting with Marilyn at her bungalow Dr. Greenson asked the star to continue the therapy sessions at his office, not far from the hotel. When Marilyn first visited the office Dr. Greenson requested she sit in a chair facing him. She was thirty- four, he, forty-eight.

As a source within his family told me, Marilyn looked at him with a question in her expressive blue eyes, then asked, "Can't I lie on the couch as I do with Dr. Kris?"

Dr. Greenson replied with reason and caution, "Let us be modest about what we want to achieve here. We don't have to make a deep change since you'll soon return to New York and your analyst there."

What they talked about that session and the following ones remains unknown. But according to the source, on Marilyn's next visit she seemed upset, as though she did not wish to speak a single word.

Finally Dr. Greenson asked, "Is anything wrong?"

She confessed, "I'm hurt because you didn't think I was 'modest.'"

At first he did not know what she meant. Then he realized she thought his use of the word "modest" meant *she* was not "modest," implying she was overly sexy and ostentatious. He had used the word modest to refer to the temporary assistance she could expect from him before returning to Dr. Kris.

Dr. Greenson assured the star that he meant the word to describe how much could be achieved during her sessions in the short time she would remain in Hollywood. She apologized for making the mistake, smiled. She reported promptly for the few successive sessions, the film was completed and she flew home to Manhattan, her husband, the playwright Arthur Miller and Dr. Kris.

After four years of marriage it had become evident any hope of continuing the marriage had ended. Miller had written a film that would star her, *The Misfits*, and there was an unspoken agreement neither would take divorce action until it was completed. Without the four years of therapy with Dr. Kris, she would not have remained with Miller as long as she did.

In the months before Marilyn left New York for Reno, where the filming would take place, she had an affair with the Danish writer

Hans Jorgen Lembourn, who later wrote *Diary of a Lover of Marilyn Monroe*. He hoped to produce movie scripts, perhaps one about her. During their brief affair, according to Lembourn, Marilyn told him, "I've had lots of love. I'm incessantly in love with someone or another. Right now, with you. But it hasn't made me a bit smarter and not happier either."

Then she confessed, "Sometimes I dream that I'm buried in sand and that I lie and wait for someone to come and dig me out. I can't do it myself."

She also spoke to Lembourn of not feeling "whole," of "personalities within" that fought with one another and turned her life into a miasma of misery. As photographer Lawrence Schiller described it, "She comes out of the dressing room Norma Jeane. When she steps in front of the camera she is Marilyn."

Marilyn felt shattered as she left for Reno in the fall. While working on scenes, she collapsed on August 6, 1960 as a result of the combination of alcohol, drugs, long fights at night with her husband and the broiling heat. She was wrapped in a wet sheet, carried to a plane and flown to the Westside Hospital in Los Angeles to recuperate.

She called Dr. Greenson and during the ten days she spent in the hospital he visited her several times. Louella Parsons wrote in her column that Marilyn "was a very sick girl, much sicker than at first believed" and under psychiatric care.

At the end of September, while she was back filming *The Misfits*, W. J. Weatherby, feature writer for England's *Manchester Guardian*, visited the Reno set. He described the experience as "like standing in a minefield among all those manic-depressive people."

When the shooting ended, Marilyn and Miller returned to Manhattan via separate planes. Marilyn kept her promise to give New York columnist Earl Wilson an exclusive story on November 11, Armistice Day. She told him her marriage was over and, as he reported in his column, "there will soon be a friendly divorce."

Less than a week later, Marilyn received the news that Clark Gable, who played her leading man *The Misfits*, had died of a heart attack. Kay Gable, pregnant with a child her husband would never see, circulated the rumor that Marilyn had contributed to Gable's death by forcing him to stand in the hot sun for hours in the Reno desert because she was always late. Feeling guilty, Marilyn became very depressed, contemplated suicide.

The night *The Misfits* had disbanded, the film completed, Marilyn sat in Reno drinking straight bourbon. She announced, "I am trying to find myself as a person. Millions of people live their entire lives without finding themselves. The best way for me is to prove to myself I am an actress."

The feared nightmare of her life came true eighteen days later on February 7, 1961. She found herself in the Payne Whitney Psychiatric Clinic of the New York Hospital-Cornell Medical Center. Dr. Kris sent her there in an effort to help her give up the powerful drugs that were turning her into a virtual zombie. It was reported Marilyn visited Dr. Kris forty-seven times in the previous two months complaining of depression and the desire to kill herself. Alarmed at Marilyn's excessive drinking, Dr. Kris now tried the Payne Whitney Clinic, noted for its treatment of the disturbed person.

Marilyn, who arrived expecting a luxurious rest cure, found herself a prisoner in the white brick skyscraper overlooking Manhattan's East River. Registered incognito as Faye Miller, she was ushered into a room on a floor reserved for the "moderately disturbed patient." Then, to her horror, all her clothes—including an expensive fur coat— were taken from the room. The door was locked from the outside. She stood aghast in a shapeless garment, all pride gone, no doubt thinking of her mother, who had spent most of her life behind locked doors in mental hospitals.

According to a Payne Whitney nurse, interviewed later by *Life* magazine, Marilyn kept screaming, "Open this door! I won't make any trouble. Just let me out! Please! Open the door!" No one came to her rescue, she felt emotionally petrified.

At this point another staff member said, Marilyn stripped naked, stood at the window gesturing for help. Finally a nurse opened the door, led Marilyn up to a security ward on the ninth floor. There, once again left alone, Marilyn attempted to escape by throwing a chair at the door, hoping it would break open and she could flee to safety.

She wrote a note to her acting coaches, Paula and Lee Strasberg, her closest friends in New York, which read (complete with misspellings):

Dear Lee and Paula,

Dr Kris has had me put into the New York Hospital—pstikiatric division under the care of two idiot doctors, they *both should not be my doctors.*

You haven't heard from me because I'm locked up with all these poor nutty people. I'm *sure* to end up a nut if I stay in this nightmare. please help me Lee, this is the *last* place I should be— maybe if you called Dr. Kris and assured her of my sensitivity and that I must get back to class...Lee, I try to remember what you said once in class, that "art goes far beyond science."

And the science memories around here I'd like to forget — like screeming women etc.

please help me — if Dr. Kris assures you I am all right you can assure her *I am not.* I do not belong here!

I love you both

Marilyn

She telephoned baseball legend and former husband Joe DiMaggio and he flew from Florida to rescue her. The evening of her third day at the Clinic, DiMaggio helped smuggle her out through a basement passageway. Those moments must have felt as exciting to her as any of her twenty-nine completed movies — *Something's Got to Give* would never be completed. Dr. Kris then sent her to the neurological department of Columbia-Presbyterian Medical Center on the other side of the city, facing the Hudson River. There Marilyn felt treated like a regular patient who needed help to give up drugs.

From this far more comforting hospital Marilyn sent a letter to Dr. Greenson that later appeared in *The Fox Archives.* Her secretary, Mary Reese, typed it from Marilyn's longhand, dispatched it to the west coast. Marilyn wrote Dr. Greenson, "Last night I was awake all night.

Sometimes I wonder what the night-time is for. It almost doesn't exist for me—it all seems like one long, long horrible day."

She added that she tried to be constructive as she read the letters of Sigmund Freud. She saw "a sad disappointment in his gentle face" but praised the fact that "his gentle, sad humor and even a striving was eternal in him."

She also wrote,"There was no empathy at Payne-Whitney— it had a very bad effect—they put me in a 'cell' (I mean those cement blocks and all) for *very disturbed* depressed patients except I felt I was in some kind of prison for a crime I hadn't comitted (her spelling). The inhumanity there I found archaic...there were screaming women in their cells."

She then observed, "Oh, well, men are climbing to the moon but they don't seem interested in the beating human heart." She also wrote, "I know I will never be happy but I know I can be gay! Remember I told you Elia Kazan said I was the gayest girl he ever knew and believe me he has known many. But he *loved* me for one year and once rocked me to sleep one night when I was in great anguish. He also suggested that I go into analysis and later wanted me to work with his teacher, Lee Strasberg." Thus Kazan was responsible for the first mention of psychoanalysis in her life and also for her friendship with the Strasberg family.

She then asked "Was it Milton who wrote: 'The happy ones were never born?' I know at least two psychiatrists who are looking for a more positive approach." In quoting this thought of Milton's she reveals the wish she had never been born.

She also said, "By the way I have some good news, sort of, since I guess I helped, he claims I did." Referring to Joe DiMaggio, she explained, "Joe said I saved his life by sending him to a psychotherapist; Dr. Kris says he is a very brilliant man, the doctor." This may well have been Dr. Greenson, since she and Dr. Greenson were friends, even though the entire width of the country separated them.

Marilyn added, "Joe said he pulled himself up by his own bootstraps after the divorce but he told me also that if he had been me he would have divorced him too."

She concluded, "I think I had better stop because you have other things to do but thanks for listening for a while," signed the letter "Marilyn M."

Then she added a postscript: "Someone when I mentioned his name you used to frown with your mustache and look up at the ceiling. Guess who? He has been (secretly) a very tender friend. I know you won't believe this but you must trust me with my instincts. It was sort of a fling on the wing. I had never done that before but now I have—but he is very unselfish in bed." Could this be a reference to Frank Sinatra, whom she saw quite often in New York at this time?

"From Yves I have heard nothing—but I don't mind since I have such a strong, tender, wonderful memory.

"I am almost weeping." ⸱

❦ ❦ ❦

Marilyn did not make one film in 1961. She suffered frequent abnormal bleeding from the uterus and had an ulcerated colon. Twice that summer she found herself in a hospital. In May she underwent a gynecological operation in Los Angeles. On signing in, Marilyn used the name her mother gave her, Norma Jean, not her screen name, as though wishing her mother were there to comfort her through this serious operation, one that would place another slash on her once-perfect body.

Doctors discovered that her Fallopian tubes were blocked as a result of inept surgery following an abortion—Marilyn once said she had undergone fourteen abortions. The guilt over this act ran high in this era and Marilyn no doubt thought of herself as a murderer, as most women did after an abortion. In society, at this time, Marilyn would thus be considered a murderer fourteen times over.

As she recovered, Marilyn called Dr. Greenson and he visited her at the hospital. She told him her marriage had ended, said she was thinking of living in Los Angeles, though also keeping her New York apartment. She asked if he would take her as a regular patient when she returned shortly to the magical territory known as Hollywood and he agreed.

One month later, on June 1, 1961, her thirty-fifth birthday, she was carried on a stretcher into the Polyclinic Hospital in New York with an acutely inflamed gall bladder. She sent Dr. Greenson a telegram: "In this world of people I'm glad there's you. I have a feeling of hope although today I am three-five." The age of thirty-five made her feel old. She would live one year and two months longer.

She kept in constant contact with Dr. Greenson. One of Marilyn's secretaries, Marjorie Stengel, who had worked for Montgomery Clift and other stars recalled that Marilyn's life "was nothing. She didn't do anything except conduct long secretive phone calls in another room, often with her analyst in California."

At this time Dr. Greenson wrote a colleague he thought Marilyn was "doing quite well." He added, however, that he was appalled at the emptiness of her life in terms of "object relations"—the ability to have a successful relationship with a loved one. He noted, "Essentially, it is such a narcissistic way of life. All in all there's been some improvement, but I do not vouch for how deep it is or how lasting."

Before leaving the hospital, as she wrote Dr. Greenson, she stood on the balcony of her room talking to Dr. Richard Cottrell, who had removed her gall bladder. Suddenly she turned to Dr. Cottrell, said, "Look at the stars. They are all up there shining so brightly but each one must be so very alone."

Marilyn then remarked to Dr. Cottrell, "It's a make-believe world, isn't it?"

These two sad remarks revealed how she felt about life. First, that she had always been "very alone." Second, that the world in which she lived was "make believe."

She projected on the stars her deepest fear—loneliness. From the day she was born she felt alone. No mother, except Saturday afternoons and even then not always. No father, ever. No grandparents. No aunts, no uncles. Only a series of foster parents. And when you live in a foster home you do not feel that either the foster parents or the house are yours. You are an outcast.

She had to pretend life was a lark to assuage her deeply buried fear and rage. Without this pretense, she could not have survived even her desolate thirty-six years. When she used the name "Norma Jean" as she signed in to face the operation, she was saying, "I feel like a little girl again and I'm scared to death."

Dr. Cottrell later told another doctor her inflammation was the result of a "chronic fear neurosis" that caused her to be highly nervous, confused and frightened.

After leaving the hospital she headed for Los Angeles and her former apartment in a building she had once lived as Norma Jean. Her small dark rooms looked out on a courtyard. She made arrangements to see Dr. Greenson five days a week. She started this analysis in earnest, urged on by Dr. Kris, who knew Marilyn wished to return to Hollywood following the devastating divorce from Miller. He was planning to marry photographer Inge Morath, whom he met during the filming of *The Misfits*.

When Dr. Greenson first saw Marilyn he listened to what he described as her "venomous resentment" of her third husband. She claimed Miller was "cold and unresponsive" to her problems, attracted to other women and dominated by his mother. Dr. Greenson met Miller and reported he was "very interested in helping his wife and sincerely concerned about her, but from time to time gets angry and rejecting." Dr. Greenson felt the playwright had "the attitude of a father who has done more than most fathers would do, and is rapidly coming to the end of his rope."

He told Miller that Marilyn demanded the impossible—love and devotion without conditions—anything less was unbearable. This would be an impossible demand for any one mortal to fulfill, the fantasy of fantasies.

One reason Marilyn may have felt at home with Dr. Greenson was that her Hollywood lawyer, Milton (Mickey) Rudin, was his brother-in-law. No doubt Rudin highly approved of Marilyn's taking on his brother-in-law as her psychoanalyst. Rudin may even have suggested this before Dr. Greenson was called by Dr. Kris in New York to talk about Marilyn.

She told Dr. Greenson, as he relayed it to a colleague, she felt continually as if she were "taking a beating, like a soldier in the war," added, "I remember things from childhood that burn in my mind."

He was aware of her desperate cry for help and the fantasies of fear and rage that frightened her, as they do all of us to some degree. The phrase she used about childhood memories that "burn in my mind," describes angry, fiery thoughts of wishes for revenge. All childhoods are traumatic at one time or another for there is no perfect childhood. Parents are not the gods children wish them to be.

According to his colleague, Dr. Greenson noted that Marilyn appeared heavily sedated, slurred her words and had poor reactions. She seemed remote, failed to understand simple conversational sallies and rambled on incoherently, though at times she also would seem "remote."

Dr. Greenson was aware of the depth of Marilyn's emotional illness but held the hope he could help her by persuading her to drastically cut the use of destructive drugs. He gambled she would not be driven through depression to a final suicidal act, knowing she had previously taken overdoses of pills, then rescued miraculously by others.

She described her lifelong inability to fall asleep at night as justifying the constant use of pills and alcohol. She told Dr. Greenson her difficulty stemmed from the nights as a child she spent in strange foster homes and an orphanage. She complained she never had a family from the day she was born, taken directly from the hospital to foster parents. She said she could not trust voices she heard in the night or figures moving about a darkened house in which she always remained the stranger, the intruder.

Dr. Greenson wrote his colleague he was amazed with her knowledge of how to obtain large doses of drugs by going from one doctor to another, never informing them of prior prescriptions. He discovered she took endless doses of Demerol, a narcotic analgesic similar to morphine. She also used the barbiturate phenobarbital HMC and Amytal as well as sodium pentothol, which depressed the nervous system. He objected to the Demerol which was very dangerous if used frequently. She habitually took several of these drugs.

He feared she was on the verge of becoming a hopeless addict. He tried to convince her she could fall asleep without drugs if tired enough. In the correspondence with this colleague, he said, "I told her that she's already received so much medication that it would put five other people to sleep, but the reason she wasn't sleeping was because she was afraid of sleeping. I promised she would sleep with less medication if she would recognize she is fighting sleep as well as searching for some obvious oblivion which is not sleep."

Dr. Greenson also spoke to his colleague of Marilyn revelling "in her personal appearance, feeling that she was an extremely beautiful woman, perhaps the most beautiful woman in the world. She always took great pains to be attractive and to give a very good appearance when she was out in public, although when she was at home and nobody could see her she might not be able to put herself together very well. She felt at times she was insignificant, unimportant."

He summed up, " The main mechanism she used to bring some feeling of stability and significance to her life was the attractiveness of her body."

This was clearly apparent in the hours she spent taking care of it. She sought experts to style her hair, put on her makeup, massage her skin for hours. The body seemed the thing by which she survived. As the body started to falter in her thirties it was as though she was betrayed by her body and as good as dead.

That her body was her emotional spine, so to speak, can clearly be seen in the way she walks in all her films. It is a walk that tells the world, I am my body, love it, love me. If you do not love my body, I am as nothing. I might as well die.

Now, with Dr. Greenson, she faced a difficult task. One that involved bringing to the conscious part of her mind long-buried feelings of terror, fear and wish for revenge on those who had hurt her as a child. Such child-borne feelings never disappear, they remain as subtle murderers of the mind, slowly building up their destructive power if we do not become consciously aware of them, make peace with them.

Dr. Greenson commented that Marilyn's continuing complaints about other people told much about her. He wrote, "As she becomes more anxious, she begins to act like an orphan, a waif, and she masochistically provokes them [people] to mistreat her and to take advantage of her."

Dr. Greenson further described her: "This thirty-five year old woman still thinks of herself as a fragile waif." She was showing the world what she suffered as a child. One of her defenses was a plea for pity and love for that fragile waif. A plea no doubt made over and over since the moment she first started to relate to another person.

🐛 🐛 🐛

The second office in which Dr. Greenson asked Marilyn to visit was located in his home in Santa Monica. He saw several patients there and he now made this decision about her, according to someone who knew him well, because he wished to make it easier for her to go unrecognized when she appeared for therapy. He shared his downtown office with the well-known psychoanalyst, Dr. Milton Wexler.

The first time Marilyn arrived at Dr. Greenson's home, via a limousine, she was almost half an hour late. Dr. Greenson asked her to try to be prompt in the future. He told her that not being punctual was a sign of dislike for the person you were meeting. That thought must have struck home for from then on she arrived early. He noticed from his desk at the window in the consultation room that she often walked up and down the street as she waited for her hour.

The Greensons lived in a spacious, very attractive white stucco house set back from the street. Green lawns stretched out in front and palm trees lined the wide road. On clear days you could see the palms on the Santa Monica palisades and, in the distance, the usually placid ocean.

Thus in 1961 the country's most popular film star and one of its most esteemed psychoanalysts joined forces to try to save the star's life. This could be called an unusual fact crime "whydunit" in that the victim was also the killer. Suicide is always murder turned on the self because of a violent rage felt toward someone else.

Unless it was raining, instead of sitting in the limousine Marilyn would take short walks until she saw the patient before her step out of the house. Then she would open the unlocked door, walk inside.

Dr. Greenson's office was smaller than his downtown office but set in a relaxing, quiet atmosphere. He would sit by the front window in a comfortable leather chair at a large wooden desk. He faced a second leather chair in which he asked Marilyn to sit. There were never papers on his desk. He worked at his scientific writings in a den upstairs.

During the year he saw Marilyn, there were no pictures of Freud on the walls, they appeared in his Beverly Hills office, Mrs. Greenson recalled. One painting still on the wall featured a woman sitting quietly, her back to the viewer, as she gazed at a garden. The ceiling directly above where Marilyn sat held wooden beams, several feet apart.

Dr. Greenson, who treated a number of men and women starring in films, was an intense, slender man, known for his sensitive and deep personal concern for patients. Of Russian parentage, he grew up in New York, then trained as a psychoanalyst in Switzerland and Vienna. When he decided to make his home in Los Angeles, he fought his battles not only with patients on the couch, as he helped them face the destructive fantasies in their unhappy lives, but also with real enemies of the United States of America.

During World War II he served as chief of the Combat Fatigue Section of the Army Air Corps. After the war he became clinical professor of psychiatry at the University of California at Los Angeles.

He now saw Marilyn five, perhaps six or even seven times a week to help her overcome her depressions. He must have realized how alone in the world she felt, had always felt, from the day of birth. If ever Dr. Greenson had a patient he pitied, it had to be Marilyn Monroe. He recognized at once what he called her "terrible loneliness," and fears that had engulfed her from childhood on.

He decided to ask his family to treat her like a member of the household so she would feel wanted by someone, provide the family she never had. She was usually the last patient of the day and he invited her, when she did not have other plans, to join his family for supper. Her personal choice for a drink was Dom Perignon champagne, which she brought from home to share.

She became like an adopted daughter in the family. His daughter Joan, and Marilyn swiftly took to each other. Dr. Greenson also encouraged his twenty-four-year old son, Daniel, to spend time with

Marilyn. He hoped the new atmosphere, plus her many sessions with him, would overcome her earliest terrors as she had found herself alone in the world.

He believed his family would help Marilyn feel more assured of her inner worth. He knew all the fame and success in the world could not heal the early scars of abandonment and loneliness. She would have to face what had caused these scars before she would feel at peace with herself.

He was aware of the depth of her need—a need that still existed—for two parents to nourish her emotionally, as well as physically. He had learned how tragic the early life of Norma Jean. He knew that even years of stardom and world fame could in no way obliterate the early tortured feelings resulting from abandonment by both parents.

As a friend of Dr. Greenson's put it, "He was an enormous optimist when it came to patients. I knew Marilyn somewhat and saw how volatile she was. Her mind could change very rapidly. She also exaggerated her emotions. She could give in quickly to anger if someone verbally attacked a friend. Such an exaggerated emotion is unreal. It was part of her sickness."

The doors of the Greenson home were open to Marilyn at any hour. She learned she was welcome in all rooms, not just the treatment one. She had free access to the kitchen, the dining room and the luxurious living room, all on the ground floor.

The living room occupied almost half of the first floor to the rear. Behind it stretched a large garden, edged by trees and flowers. The walls were wood-paneled, with beams overhead. One side of the room included a wide balcony. Below it, on a wall, there was a Max Band painting titled "Displaced Person." It featured the face of a very depressed man. This contrasted with a more cheerful second Band painting next to it, featuring peaches and cherries.

The Greensons had a love of Spanish Monterey architecture, clearly shown in the huge fireplace with magnificent hand-made tiles of vivid colors, imported from Mexico. The tiles spread down the two sides of the fireplace, then low along each wall for several yards. Marilyn became so enamoured of them that when she bought her own home nearby in February, 1962 she flew to Mexico to order tiles for her living room. They also appeared in the Greensons' large kitchen, giving it a warm, sumptuous feeling.

The linen drapes in the Greensons' living room were of green and brown geometric patterns. An antique wooden table sat squarely in front of the huge fireplace. Almost across the side of one wall spread an ancient walnut table, resembling those once used by monks. Visitors enjoyed the room's subdued elegance and silent beauty. If anyone wished to read, two bookcases lined one wall. There was also a grand piano to accompany Dr. Greenson, who played the violin, as he invited groups of friends who enjoyed making music.

Marilyn often curled up in a blue velvet chair and listened to the classical rhythms. One night she brought a dear friend from New York, led him into the living room and announced proudly, "This is where we have chamber music."

Another evening Mrs. Greenson saw Marilyn sitting near a window, listening, her head lowered, swinging her hand to the music. Mrs. Greenson recalled, "By the movement of her hand I had the feeling she was almost dancing."

Dr. Greenson chose Mrs. Eunice Murray to look after Marilyn as her companion and house-keeper. Mrs. Murray was, as his friends put it, "a very quiet, unobtrusive woman who would not impose herself on anyone. Marilyn could not stand an opinionated person and enjoyed Eunice's peaceful manner."

Mrs. Greenson spoke of her feelings for Marilyn when I visited her. She said she admired and liked Marilyn very much. She added, "When you saw her move, there was something intriguing and original about the way she used her body. It seemed almost a put-on, a parody of her own walking."

Both Mrs. Greenson's daughter and son enjoyed Marilyn's company. She recalled Danny once saying, "Good Lord, who would believe I just left home for the evening, where Marilyn was peeling potatoes as I gave her a peck on the cheek." He described her as "in no way put on or artificial, she had real warmth." Today Dr. Daniel Greenson is a psychoanalyst living in Berkeley, California.

Marilyn endeared herself to the household by insisting on helping them cook supper and clean up afterward. She said, "I do dishes very well. I learned how in the foster homes and the orphanage." Mrs. Greenson, who lives alone in the house today, said Marilyn held a natural attraction for people even when she went without makeup, did not dress up and they did not recognize her.

Mrs. Greenson recalled driving Marilyn home and stopping for gas. The employees were not aware this was Marilyn but asked with interest, "What are you girls doing later?" Mrs. Greenson described Marilyn as "true honey, she attracted all men. She did nothing, just sat there."

Once when Joan was driving Marilyn in a convertible and Marilyn's hair was waving in the breeze, a truck driver pulled up parallel to them trying to make a date and when he got no response he called out, "Who the hell do you think you are—Marilyn Monroe?" Then he drove away fast, an indignant look on his face.

"Even her presence had an aura," Mrs. Greenson said. "People were naturally attracted to her." There were times though when Mrs. Greenson, as she put it, "had my worries and doubts about Marilyn. I saw how volatile she could be, how her mind could change very rapidly. Joan had a friend who one day acted meanly to her and she told Marilyn this. Marilyn became unduly outraged. It seemed an exaggerated emotion, as many of her feelings were."

Joan Greenson Aebi, who today lives in Pasadena, had just turned twenty-one when she met Marilyn. Joan was in her first year of study at the Otis Art Institute in the mid-Wilshire area of Los Angeles.

Joan recalls that when her father told her Marilyn Monroe would be pulling up in a car on the street outside their house in the late afternoons on weekdays, she would peek out between the curtains in her room on the second floor to see the famous star leave the limousine.

Dr. Greenson taught once a week at the University of California in Los Angeles and when he knew he might be late, asked Joan to take a short walk with Marilyn rather than let her sit in the limousine. Joan said that when she was a child and patients visited the house, she was not allowed to play in the front yard—"when they appeared I was taught it was time to disappear." She adds, "But not when Marilyn became a patient. Then my father encouraged me to greet her at the door and take walks with her until he arrived."

She said that when her father suggested this, "I was excited and nervous. I was an art student—what was I going to say to her?"

She recalls her first impression of Marilyn as one of "fascination." Marilyn had just finished making *The Misfits*. Once, during filming Marilyn stayed with her husband at the Beverly Hills Hotel. Feeling ill, she called Dr. Greenson, who went to the hotel, then called Joan, asked her to pick up a prescription he had ordered at a nearby drug store and bring it to him. Joan did so, knocked on the door of the room her father had asked her to deliver it.

"Marilyn was lying in bed and I only saw her arm but I did see Arthur Miller," Joan says. "That was a big deal to me."

Joan adds, "I learned a lot from Marilyn, for which I am grateful. I learned it was okay to be a sexual person. Part of my teenage rebellion was to be uptight."

Marilyn was "very sweet and worldly but in some ways she wasn't educated. She had never allowed herself to be a teenager, to learn the way of teendom."

She added,"When I first met her she overwhelmed me. I had never met anyone like her. She possessed a quality that I would call almost feline-like. She also seemed totally at home with her own body. She let her emotions come through her body.

"What made her different, I wondered? Why do we worship her? There was something unique about her that caused you to watch her carefully, as though she was one of a kind, very precious."

When Joan first started to take walks with Marilyn, "it was overwhelming—the difference between what she was and what I was. I saw all the stereotypes about her were not true, that she was breathless and gushy, she was only that way when she played the part of Marilyn Monroe.

"I found it fascinating to walk and talk with her. It was exciting though at the same time it undid me. I was aware I was in the presence of a great star. I had met other movie people in our home but I never had this 'wow!' feeling about anyone."

She describes her year-long relationship with Marilyn as "strange" in that "many times I reacted as if she was an older sister though sometimes the roles were reversed as I became the older sister and she learned from me."

Joan adds she "was not aware of Marilyn's reaction to me but she was careful not to shock me through language and what she was doing in her life, whom she dated."

It was not difficult "to perceive how unhappy Marilyn was," Joan said. Sometimes she would call the house and talking in a thick tongue, as though drunk, ask, "Can I speak to Dr. Greenson?"

"You could see and feel her unhappiness," Joan added. "Not only her neurosis but who she was made her a total prisoner."

Joan also spoke of the "mystery of Marilyn...the very aura of the way in which Marilyn moved, the extremely sensuous way she walked. It was more than a walk, it wasn't just wiggly hips, for even when she was sitting you were aware of her body, it seemed to flow. There was never a dancer so at home with her body. Beauty radiated from it, it told of a quality of stardom in just the space she took up. She was totally at home with her body."

In contrast Joan adds, "Yet there was also a feeling of great sorrow about her. You could feel it as you looked at her."

One evening Dr. Greenson's quartet played a Mozart quintet as Marilyn sat in the wingback chair, listening ardently. Joan recalls that Marilyn slowly started to allow her body to move to the timing of the music, as the feelings increased in intensity. Joan said, "Marilyn was totally engrossed, not aware of her moves. I thought I had no business being part of this because it was so intensely personal. I felt I was a voyeur, a Peeping Tom. It was truly a memorable moment."

She admits that at times Marilyn "wasn't easy to get along with. She never saw things except in black and white which made a relationship tenuous, though never with me. Sometimes she argued strongly with others and they were dead in the water if they disagreed, as far as she was concerned."

Joan had faith her father could help Marilyn. She pointed out that Marilyn had come a long way in the first half year she was treated by Dr. Greenson. He encouraged her to buy her own home. Marilyn had never owned a piece of property and this took courage. Joan says, "It was interesting to listen to her having more of a life of her own."

Since Marilyn had sought him out, Dr. Greenson decided to try to help her. No doubt he sensed it might be a losing battle but he was determined to do his best in the treatment room where she spoke of her traumas and he also offered in a generous gesture his family as substitute for the one she never had.

Some psychoanalysts thought he never should have let her become close to his family but treat her as he did all the rest of his patients. He later told a colleague that he believed if he had committed her to a mental hospital she would have taken her life even sooner.

The obvious facts of Marilyn's short life and the many men with whom she had affairs starting at the age of eighteen are well-known. It is the *fantasies* of her life that have never been described. Fantasies connected to these facts. For it is our fantasies from birth on, perhaps even starting "in utero," as psychoanalysts believe, that may drive us to self-destruct. As they literally did Marilyn.

Millions of readers throughout the world could not believe their eyes as they read the newspaper headline on Monday, April 6, 1962: MARILYN MONROE COMMITS SUICIDE.

Why would she take her own life? She had everything—international fame, money, all the men she wished. She had reached the very pinnacle of her acting career in her film *The Misfits*. In the fall of 1962 she was to star in *Something's Got to Give* with Dean Martin, who admired her.

Yet two months into her thirty-sixth year she preferred to die by her own hand rather than continue climbing in her established, gratifying profession.

Almost every author of a book about Marilyn has stressed her addiction to alcohol and barbiturates as the immediate cause of her death, except for the few who believe someone murdered her, ranging from the Kennedys to the Mafia bosses as the killers. But no one has explained Marilyn's deep-seated need to become addicted. Or dealt with the inner demons that drove her to the final overdose that snuffed out her life. No one has described in detail the connection between her early crippling childhood and the growing intensity of the fear, fury and anguish that caused her many suicide attempts, culminating in a final one that succeeded.

Why did she decide to end it all? What were the grim realities as she saw them? And the even more grim fantasies whirling in her mind over the years, that drove her to such an early death? What were the many tortures that finally overcame her will to live?

Dr. Greenson had taken a chance. She had sought him after four years of psychoanalysis with Dr. Kris, during which Marilyn must have felt some relief from the agony of the many demons pursuing her in her dreams and real life. He gambled on the idea that giving her a home with a family for the first time in her life might raise her sunken spirit.

At this point Marilyn openly could not cope with her growing fears. Too many suicide attempts. Too many abortions. Too many men as lovers. But even at this late date she did not give up. She wished to make one last attempt to conquer the ghosts of the past. Ghosts too powerful for her to face alone.

As Joan Greenson said, "In the long haul, I don't think Marilyn had any chance to survive. She was too fragile emotionally. She should be honored for having gone as far as she did."

As she started therapy with Dr. Greenson, Marilyn faced life's most difficult task, bringing to the conscious part of her mind the long, deeply buried feelings of terror, fear and wish for revenge on those who had hurt her as a child.

Such feelings never disappear. They remain as subtle murderers of the mind, slowly building up their destructive power if we do not become aware of how dangerous they are.

Marilyn managed to muster the courage to seek Dr. Greenson, hoping he would swiftly understand all that had gone awry in her life. He possessed the courage to accept her challenge. She would try to understand why she felt "buried in sand," as she told Lembourn, with Dr. Greenson's aid.

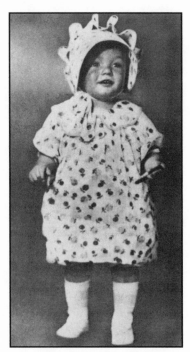

Norma Jean at 2
© Robert F. Slatzer

2.
Sex as Survival

The lonely thirty-five year old woman who sat facing Dr. Greenson in the office at his home during the fall of 1961 revealed secrets of her life she had never dared tell anyone. Nor could Dr. Greenson ever disclose what those secrets were for his profession forbid this.

It is a stringent law of psychoanalysis that the psychoanalyst never divulge one word of a patient to anyone. Mrs. Greenson said her husband did not take notes. Most analysts do not, except for occasional brief memos to themselves about something the patient said which they may later wish to interpret for him. Or, if an analyst does keep notes, at his death they are all destroyed.

Dr. Greenson must have marveled that Marilyn had come as far as she did, given her traumatic childhood. He knew her unhappy life was not enhanced one whit by her worldwide success as a sex symbol and comic actress. Rather, it was slowly shaken to its darkest core as she realized success and money did not lessen her gruesome fantasies.

Dr. Greenson's sympathetic approach and brilliant mind grasped the depth of Marilyn's despair. He tried to convince her, as he later told one colleague, to give up both her precious champagne and vodka and the cascade of sleeping pills she poured into herself nightly. At times he succeeded but in the long run he would lose the battle.

Dr. Greenson was known throughout the world of psychoanalysis as a man of originality, contributing much research to the field. Charles F. Ehrhardt, a New York psychotherapist, says Dr. Greenson's book *The Technique and Practice of Psychoanalysis* is one of three that are essential to helping analysts "truly understand the mechanisms of analysis inside out." He names the other two as Freud's *The Interpretation of Dreams* and Otto Fenichel's *Psychoanalytic Theory of the Neurosis.*

Ehrhardt says further of *The Technique and Practice of Psychoanalysis*, "It is very lucid, gives many examples and his style is uncomplicated. He writes free of cliché and professional jargon. He makes the process of analysis seem a process between two human beings. You sense his concern for the patient."

Dr. Greenson was known for his emphasis on the importance of the analyst showing empathy toward the patient. No analysis could be successful, he believed, if the psychoanalyst lacked this quality. Only as the patient felt he was understood, liked, respected, could he give up the traumas of childhood.

Dr. Greenson had friendly brown eyes and a reassuring voice. A moving personal description was given by Paul Moor, international journalist, musician, critic of music and plays and author of *The Self Portrait of Jürgen Bartsche,* a powerful study of a young serial murderer published in Germany in 1972. Paul has remained a close friend of Mrs. Greenson and Joan.

Paul met Dr. Greenson—"Romi," as his close friends called him— in 1971 at the first Vienna meeting of the International Psychoanalytical Association. For twelve years Paul served as Berlin correspondent for *Time* magazine, filed stories on cultural events. In his spare time he wrote musical and theatrical reviews for the *Times* in London and the *Herald Tribune* in Paris.

Dr. Fredrick J. Hacker, a friend of Paul's, was also attending the historic Vienna meeting and invited him to dinner. Dr. Hacker explained first he would stop at the Hotel Sacher to pick up Dr. Greenson and his wife. Paul was delighted, he had read Dr. Greenson's classic book and most of his professional articles. Paul had been in analysis in New York for nine months before moving to Europe. He lived in Paris from 1949 to 1951, in Munich from 1951 to 1956 and in Berlin from 1956 to 1981, when he returned to the United States.

For seven years Paul attended the training program of the Berlin Psychoanalytic Institute, the world's first psychoanalytic institute. He did not intend to practice but was admitted to the "theoretical services." He started private psychoanalytic sessions in Berlin with Dr. Felix Boehm, after the latter's death continued with Dr. Bruno May.

Dr. Hacker drove Dr. Greenson, his wife and Paul in his Mercedes convertible to a *Heuriger* (wine house) in the suburb of Grinzing where they enjoyed dinner in the garden, drank wine. Paul kept silent, listened to the two older men. But when Dr. Greenson learned Paul was an accomplished musician, had attended the Julliard School of Music in New York, earned a degree, he "opened up like a flower," as Paul describes it. The two talked at length the rest of the evening about the world of music they loved.

Paul later learned Dr. Greenson had studied medicine in Bern, Switzerland, then started his psychoanalytic studies in Vienna with the famed Dr. Wilhelm Stekel. Dr. Greenson continued his analysis in Los Angeles with Dr. Otto Fenichel, one of the original psychoanalysts who worked with Freud.

Paul met Dr. Greenson a second time two years later when he drove to the Paris airport to pick up the doctor and his wife. They were all attending the 1973 yearly meeting of the International Psychoanalytical Association. Norman Mailer's book on Marilyn Monroe had just appeared. Dr. Greenson told Paul he had expressed surprise to Mailer when he contacted him after reading the book because he thought he might have helped Mailer understand Marilyn better. The appearance of Mailer's book led to Dr. Greenson's first mention of Marilyn in Paul's presence.

Paul then asked Dr. Greenson a question about his technique with Marilyn, which Paul explained he had wanted to ask after reading Fred Guiles' book *Legend: The Life and Death of Marilyn Monroe*. Guiles depicted Dr. Greenson as having virtually made Marilyn a member of the Greenson family. Paul thought this a "wildly improbable, totally anti-analytic approach to therapy." He fully expected Dr. Greenson to deny this.

Paul recalls, "Instead, with wide eyes, Romi said, 'But that's exactly what I did do!'"

Dr. Greenson explained further, "More than anything else in the world at that point she needed the sort of warmth and affection a happy, well integrated family could give her. Something she had never had in her life, and something she couldn't find now, anywhere else, because of her celebrity."

Dr. Greenson also explained to Paul why all his friends called him "Romi." At birth in Brooklyn, his mother had named him "Romeo" and his twin sister "Juliet." During school days his classmates teased him so unmercifully about the romantic name he decided to change it to "Ralph." But friends and family still called him "Romi," adapted from Romeo.

Guiles and other writers quoted Marilyn as referring to Dr. Greenson behind his back as "Romi" but Dr. Greenson told Paul she always called him Dr. Greenson to his face.

Paul believes that Dr. Kris and Dr. Greenson conferred for a considerable length of time by long distance phone between New York and Los Angeles as Dr. Kris described Marilyn's emotional conflicts, her excessive drinking and non-stop pill-taking.

The last Christmas of Marilyn's life, in 1961, she brought Joe DiMaggio, whom she still saw occasionally, to the Greensons' home. While few could upstage her, Joe did, as the two men of the house, father and son, both rabid sports fans, zeroed in on DiMaggio, discussed his past games, recalled exciting hits and players, Mrs. Greenson said. Marilyn sat in silence, listening. She may have been remembering the one Christmas she enjoyed with her mother in their own home, when she was eight, a month before her mother left her forever for the mental hospitals.

Mrs. Greenson also said of Marilyn, "Some of the most beautiful people cannot believe they are desirable. Marilyn was one."

Paul recalled that this echoes what he heard Dr. Greenson say in German during an interview with a television team from Berlin. Dr. Greenson emphasized that he spoke not specifically about Marilyn but a certain type of woman.

Over the years Paul made annual trips to America, sometimes visited the Greensons. He dined at their home in the spring of 1972, stayed with them a few days in 1974. As far as he knew, he says, Dr. Greenson did not play the piano only the violin "though they had a fine Bechstein grand in their living room."

He added, "Romi may have been the world's worst violinist because he obstinately refused to practice *at all*, in spite of organizing frequent evenings of chamber music in his home. These sometimes got quite ambitious. I remember playing one of Bach's Brandenburg Concertos on one occasion. That requires more than just a handful of participants."

One time Paul brought his copy of *The Technique and Practice of Psychoanalysis* all the way to Santa Monica for Dr. Greenson to inscribe. Paul recalls, "My chest swells perceptibly when I remember what Romi wrote in it on July 11, 1972: 'For my dear friend Paul the Moor of Berlin—fellow musician, and Analytiker. With warm feelings, Romi.'" *Analytiker* is the German word for psychoanalyst.

Marilyn taught Joan how to apply makeup, walk in a sexual manner, dance the latest steps. Paul points out that Joan had met famous people, such as Anna Freud and Margaret Mead, was not awed by celebrities.

Dr. Greenson suggested Marilyn hire Mrs. Eunice Murray, primarily to drive her to and from her apartment in Doheny Drive, and then later in January, 1962 when she bought the house, from Brentwood to Dr. Greenson's home. But, more important, he wanted someone in Marilyn's home during the day to help her through difficult times and alert him to any sudden need to see him on weekends, no matter the hour.

Guiles describes Mrs. Murray "as self-effacing as Marilyn." She did not wish to be called a housekeeper and did not pretend to have the qualifications of a psychiatric nurse though she had once cared for several slightly emotionally disturbed women. For Marilyn she carried out such tasks as answering the door or phone, cleaning and dusting, as well as driving the car. Once an excellent driver, Marilyn no longer wished to be at the wheel.

No matter how hard Dr. Greenson tried to rescue Marilyn from her misery, as he told Paul, he realized he could only aid by helping her slowly understand what tormented her. He faced the fact, as his remarks to a colleague revealed, that first he had to help her give up both alcohol and pills before she could speak of her inner torment.

Other psychoanalysts might have given up but he decided to fight against odds that were awesome. To his everlasting credit, he tried, as perhaps few psychoanalysts would, to save Marilyn from the fate she most feared—the unbearable torture of being confined for life in a mental hospital. He knew of her childhood torments, realized she was not ready as yet to face them.

He believed she would profit emotionally from the chance to live in a home of her own, complete with swimming pool, not the dismal Doheny Drive apartment she occupied. She at last realized home ownership with her new, small one-story house at 12305 Fifth Helena Drive, in the wooded area of Brentwood. It did not match the magnificence of the usual film star's mansion but she felt proud of her first real home. She spent months furnishing it, buying many of its contents in Mexico, modeling it after the Greensons' house.

She described the new home as "a fortress where I can be safe from the world." Her use of the word "fortress" tells us she felt at war with the world and that the world was at war with her. This also describes how she felt as a little girl without a mother or father.

Marilyn, who had traveled almost around the world at times, now undertook a new kind of journey. A journey with a psychoanalyst into the unknown thoughts within her. She described him to friends as her "Jesus," believed he would save her. She fought hard at first to keep from falling into her hidden mists of agony and fury, tried to control the amount of Dom Perignon and vodka she drank every day and evening, as well as to give up a portion of the nembutal pills she swallowed to call on sleep.

❦ ❦ ❦

Marilyn told Lembourn, "I really can't stand men," when she drove South with him for a short vacation before heading west to appear in

The Misfits. She now confessed to Dr. Greenson her sexual desire diminished after she had known a man for a short while.

She was in a sense the reversal in sex of what is called the "Don Juan" syndrome, as she wandered from man to man (in Don Juan's case it was woman to woman). Marilyn was saying that after she first enjoyed the much-coveted primary sex encounter, she was driven to discard the man because every man stood for the first man in her life—the man who had refused to admit she was his child, her biological father. The man she would inevitably hate with a passion for forsaking her. She once said she wanted to meet her father one day, not tell him who she was until she had seduced him, then see the shock and horror on his face.

At first Marilyn acted out her intense sexual desire, believing it was love. Actually it was either a passing passion or a way of promoting her career when she first started out.

She felt pride at her list of conquests of men who were famous. It began with film producer Joseph Schenck, followed by Johnny Hyde, leading agent for the stars. Then DiMaggio, baseball superman, followed by Arthur Miller, playwright supreme. Along the way she fell in love with many other men between husbands, at times during her marriages. Still others she serviced for business purposes. Marilyn told Dr. Greenson she decided to move to New York at the end of 1954 when Milton Greene had set up Marilyn Monroe Productions, Inc., designed to give her artistic control and the chance to show her dramatic skills. At this time Lee Strasberg, to whom she was introduced by Elia Kazan and Cheryl Crawford, founders of the Actors Studio, convinced Marilyn to enter psychoanalysis on a long-term basis, realizing her need.

As artistic director of the Actors Studio, Strasberg had gained worldwide recognition for "The Method" style of acting. Paula, his wife, the Studio coach, guided Marilyn through the rest of her films, starting with *Bus Stop* in 1956.

Marilyn was reported to have seen a few analysts before Strasberg insisted she go to Dr. Kris, who had a worldwide reputation, telling Marilyn she could not study acting with him unless she started therapy at once with Dr. Kris.

In *Anna Freud, A Biography*, Elisabeth Young-Bruehl, describes Marianne Kris's life in Vienna, the city where she was born. Her father, Dr. Oscar Rie, a pediatrician, played cards with Freud every Saturday night in a game called "tarok." Marianne's mother was an accomplished artist. The Freud family sometimes spent parts of the summer with the Rie family in the nearby mountains.

As a child Marianne became a close friend of Anna Freud, decided early in life she wished to be a psychoanalyst like Anna and her famous father. Freud was always sympathetic to women who wanted to be analysts, encouraged them to become analyzed. He did not believe that becoming a doctor first helped, but rather hindered the understanding of the human mind.

Freud analyzed Rie's two daughters—Margarethe, the elder, who became an actress, and Marianne. Ernst Kris, who married Marianne, started out as an art historian, then decided to follow his wife into the world of psychoanalysis. He was analyzed by the noted Dr. Helene Deutsch.

When World War II started to erupt in 1938, the Nazis threatened Vienna and Freud and his family fled to England where the Kris's were treating patients. Ernst became Anna's consultant on questions of scholarship, supplied her with all her bibliographic references, organized and clarified her manuscripts, according to Young-Bruehl. Ernst also shared the editorship with Dr. Robert Waelder of the famed *Imago*, the journal that published Freud's continuous exploration of the unconscious part of the mind.

Joseph Kennedy, then the American ambassador to the Court of St. James, helped Ernst and Marianne, among other analysts, move to New York—an irony of fate, in view of Marianne's later becoming Marilyn Monroe's analyst and learning she was involved sexually with Joseph Kennedy's son, Jack, soon to be President of the United States. Ernst organized the famous yearly journal, *The Psychoanalytic Study of the Child*. He kept in constant touch with Anna, sent her shipments of American fountain pens which, she said, she liked far more than the British ones for writing articles.

In addition to treating men and women patients, both Marianne and Ernst also established children's projects at the famous *Yale Child Study Center* and became highly respected in the American Psychoanalytic Association. The two Kris children, Anna and Anton, also became psychoanalysts.

When Anna Freud visited America in the 1960s, according to Young-Bruehl, she discussed problems "with her old friends, particularly Marianne Kris and Heinz Hartmann, and with her new ones, particularly Romi Greenson," who had organized a fund for psychoanalytic research in Los Angeles. After Anna made a "wonderful trip to California in 1950 and enjoyed the hospitality extended by Greenson and his Swiss-born wife, Hildi," she wrote, "I find it quite difficult to imagine Los Angeles without me in it."

Marianne tried to convince the American Psychoanalytic Association that "the second-class citizenship" accorded institutionally to child analysts should cease. She realized this was connected to the old question of "lay analysis," since many child analysts had not gone to medical school. She claimed child analysis had become "a veritable stepchild" of the psychoanalytic institutes.

Ernst died in New York during February, 1957 at the age of fifty-six. Marianne assumed his position on the editorial board of *The Psychoanalytic Study of the Child*. In 1962, she called together a group of child analysts, suggested they start *The American Association for Child Analysis*. Marianne reported to Anna Freud, "This was one of the most exhausting weeks I went through but by now I have recovered from it."

Anna had founded *The Hampstead Child Therapy Course and Clinic* for "study group" status. This London Clinic later received a quarter of Marilyn's estate. She left the bequest to Marianne in a will just before she started treatment with Dr. Greenson, instructing Dr. Kris to give the money to the charity of her choice.

In the last letter Anna wrote Dr. Greenson, she agreed the work of Heinz Kohut, once a member of their circle, had become "anti- psychoanalytic," asked, "What will happen to psychoanalysis in the future and where will its backbone be when our generation is gone?"

In the years before Dr. Greenson's death—after Marilyn died he was repeatedly hospitalized with the heart condition which caused his death on November 24, 1979—Anna and he corresponded about producing a documentary film on the Hampstead Clinic that Dr. Greenson insisted was needed for effective fund-raising. He did not live to carry through on his generous plan to screen the film throughout California.

Anna, learning of his death, had sent a statement to his Memorial Service saying she missed Dr. Greenson. She added, "We are raising new generations of psychoanalysts all over the world. Nevertheless, we have not yet discovered the secret of how to raise the real followers of people like Romi Greenson, namely, men and women who make use of psychoanalysis to its very limits: for the understanding of themselves; of their fellow beings; for communicating with the world at large; in short, for a way of living."

When Marilyn died Anna Freud wrote Dr. Kris, "I am terribly sorry about Marilyn Monroe. I know exactly how you feel because I had exactly the same thing happen with a patient of mine who took cyanide two days before I came back from America a few years ago."

Marianne had endured tortuous operations on her hip and various episodes with her heart but had seemed active at the second Hampstead Symposium, which she attended in London in 1980. In spite of keeping her heart under control with frequent doses of nitroglycerin, the morning after the last day of the meetings she died in Martha Freud's bedroom. This was almost twenty-nine years to the day Martha, Freud's wife, had died there.

Anna Freud walked to the lunch table where Jeanne Lampl-de-Groot and Muriel Gardiner, both well-known psychoanalysts, were seated, told them of Marianne's death. She insisted the lunch proceed. Young-Bruehl wrote, "The public stoicism that Anna Freud mustered for the loss of her oldest and most maternal friend, her childhood playmate, was proportionate to the pain she felt—a compounded pain, for she had to bear it without Dorothy Burlingham," another close friend she had lost.

She also told old friends of Marianne's who had written to say they did not know what they would do without Marianne's presence, her telephone calls, her gracious, warm understanding, "It is astonishing how many other people, friends, patients, colleagues, students feel as we do. I often said to Marianne that she spent too much time on the telephone. But now I understand very well what those telephone talks meant to other people."

She had added, "I miss her very much. She was my best friend as I grew up as a child. Sometimes I pretend that she is still in New York and I only have to wait for the next opportunity to see her."

A number of people remember Dr. Kris well. Edith Atkin, wife of the late Dr. Samuel Atkin, noted psychoanalyst, saw Marianne in New York on and off from the early 1940s until she died. Mrs. Atkin, author of two books, *Part-Time Father* and *In Praise of Marriage*, told me, "I knew Marianne socially as a guest in my home when she came to dinner parties. She was the essence of kindness, not in the sentimental way but as a truly compassionate, understanding, tolerant person. She loved, adored, admired and respected her husband Ernst. You would think she was a humble housewife in the presence of a superior being."

Sometimes Marianne invited the Atkins to their summer home in Stamford. Marianne had consulted Dr. Atkin when she and Ernst first arrived in America. "Both were grateful to Sam for helping to refer patients to them," Mrs. Atkin said. At that time Dr. Atkin was Executive Director of the New York Psychoanalytic Institute.

"I also knew Marianne professionally," Mrs. Atkin recalled. "She became a consultant to the Child Development Center in New York when Dr. Peter Neubauer was director. I was then in charge of the Mental Health Consultation Unit for day-care centers and nursery schools. From time to time I sat in on Marianne's lectures to the nursery school teachers at the Center. Although I was an experienced clinical social worker, I always came away from these stimulating lectures enriched in knowledge and techniques."

Dr. Paul Brauer, a prominent member of the New York Psychoanalytic Institute, recalled Dr. Kris when she was a member of the Institute and taught incoming candidates, of which he was one. He said, "She was always gentle and understanding, very supportive of the candidates."

Dr. Arnold Richards, well-known psychoanalyst, who knew Dr.

Kris when he started to practice at the New York Psychoanalytic Institute, said that whenever he received a referral from her, it felt as if she "was entrusting to you someone to whom she expected to give deep interest, concern and dedication, almost like a mother." Dr. Kris held deep respect for young psychoanalysts, particularly in the treatment of a difficult person like Marilyn.

Robert Stewart, senior editorial vice president and publisher of his own imprints at Charles Scribner's Sons, knew Dr. Kris well as a friend. Over the years he has also done research in child development and child analysis. In an interview Mr. Stewart said openly, "I adored Marianne Kris. There was no vanity in her. She had a pleasant, warm, loving voice. She was unpretentious, never took herself seriously."

"Marilyn must have found a genuine mother surrogate in Marianne Kris, who was perhaps the first person in her troubled life to be somewhat of a mother to her," he added.

He believed, "in the best sense of the word 'love' my guess is that Marianne felt genuine love for Marilyn but kept the boundaries as an analyst should. Marilyn wanted to dominate, as she did her whole life, then felt a fear of her destructiveness and retreated.

"It was obvious Marilyn had enormous self-identity problems. In her early life she had no father and practically no mother. Marianne, in a sense, was the only mother Marilyn ever had. Leaving part of her estate to Marianne was a sign of indebtedness. Somehow Dr. Kris had the capacity to move Marilyn and show affection for her in a realistic, believable way."

Dr. Kris "treated both adults and children and understood both," Mr. Stewart said. "When she made the decision to send Marilyn to Payne-Whitney, I suspect she felt Marilyn was doing herself harm, could not function on her own at this time and that whatever was going on within her could no longer be handled. Dr. Kris had to vary the rules, she knew she was not dealing with a normal neurotic.

"Dr. Kris and Dr. Greenson in a sense had to put back or supply what should have originally been there as Marilyn grew up. She suffered such an early fragmented self-structure that she would need long-term psychological help."

Mr. Stewart said he thought that "Dr. Greenson from the beginning was never quite so committed to orthodox techniques as many of his colleagues were. He believed in 'empathy' with the patient and his enemies were quick to believe his treatment failed to help her.

"It was very difficult to deal with someone like Marilyn, who was so fragmented, so deprived, lacking early love and the true mothering every child needs. Dr. Kris had a gentleness and a grasp of what effective analysis was. It's always much easier to blame somebody than to assume they did some good. Maybe we still have to need to know more before we can make any final conclusion on what happened between them."

Dr. Kris reportedly called the Payne Whitney incident with Marilyn a serious error on her part as a psychoanalyst. Shortly after, Marilyn moved to Los Angeles and started treatment with Dr. Greenson. She still believed in the "rescue" fantasy that would magically lift the pain of the past, from birth on.

❦ ❦ ❦

Although Marilyn tried all her life to manipulate men, she sometimes failed, as in the case of her last marriage. She yearned for the loving, full attention of a man but even negative attention was preferable to lack of attention. Conquest of a man was something Marilyn enjoyed for a while, though it never included quietly cherishing one man for the rest of her life. Such a mature love endures, whereas "conquest" soon evaporates, demands more and more temporary sexual objects.

The Sex Goddess of the world easily achieved many conquests with her soft, inviting voice in speech and song. Her provocative walk invited sexual escapades. Her dresses exposed her perfect breasts, clung to a body always naked underneath, a body that invited acts of seduction. Marilyn epitomized sex onscreen and off. In private life she seemed to possess an unquenchable need for physical closeness with one man after another. Sometimes two or three at a time, unknown to each other.

Dr. Greenson undoubtedly pointed out to Marilyn that a sense of conquest is not a sign of mature love, as proved by the short duration of her affairs, except for the four years with Miller, during which she was continuously seeing Dr. Kris.

Dr. Greenson would have been aware of what caused her excessive need for passion and promiscuity—sex to Marilyn, as to many if not most men and women, was erroneously equated with love. A man's arms around her, his body held close and intimate, meant in her fantasy he adored and worshipped her, wanted her forever for his own.

She needed his adulation almost daily to strengthen a sense of self that had been shaky since birth. Sex was as essential to her as eating. Sex was food for the fantasies that threatened to overwhelm her, would send her to a madhouse, as they did her mother. Unless someone loved her, she would feel a "nobody" (no body), so she made her body the most alluring in the world. If men found her sexually desirable she would not go crazy as her mother did after she could not find a permanent man though she searched eight years.

Marilyn could not tolerate being "a woman scorned" as both her mother and she had been when the man by whom Gladys became pregnant refused to marry her. Unconsciously Marilyn emulated what she believed the masculine approach to sex when she became the one to "dump" the partner. As she did her first husband, Jim Dougherty, followed by Robert Slatzer, after a three-day marriage, then DiMaggio, after nine months. With Miller, though she remained over four years, it reached the point where both wished to end the misery. The few times a man walked out on her she could barely function.

She confessed she became depressed when she menstruated, a time she always suffered acute cramps. The latter occur in women who resent the monthly period, dislike being women, rebel against what they call the "curse" that reveals what they consider their frailties. Marilyn was reported at times walking around with monthly bloodstains showing through the back of her dress, as though she were a little girl waiting for her mother to "clean" her up, lessen the pain of an unwanted flow of blood.

A recent book by James Haspiel, illustrated with more than 150 color and black and white photographs he took, shows Marilyn's ethereal beauty. He describes his relationship to her as both photographer and friend, cites personal letters from her during the last eight years of her life. He first saw her in New York when she filmed *The Seven Year Itch*, met her two years later as she moved to New York.

He writes in *Marilyn: The Ultimate Look at the Legend*, that she possessed "a zest for life." She told him, "I remember when I was a kid at the movies on Saturday afternoon. I'd sit in the front row and I'd think how wonderful it would be to be an actress." This, more than any other feeling, would set her on the way to success.

Haspiel speaks of his own difficult childhood, making clear the basis for his strong empathy with Marilyn's painful growing up. When she first came to New York to live, she stayed for a while at the Waldorf Towers in a small apartment and he describes the large painting of Abraham Lincoln that hung above her bed and her continued search for more and more knowledge.

"I always felt that special bonding with Marilyn that all 'displaced' persons might inevitably experience with one another," he said. "But, as we would both eventually know, survival can be achieved." He notes, "As it had been in her life, so it was true of mine, that I was 'farmed out,' as it were, living my first seven years in other people's homes; people usually bent on treating 'the outsider' as such, therefore effectively denying me, and before me, Norma Jeane, any foundation that might give us any real sense of belonging."

He believes that Marilyn's miscarriage of her son in August, 1957 was "the closest she ever came to achieving motherhood—an already formed infant." He visited her at Doctors Hospital the day after she lost the baby. He points out that five years later she would kill herself on August 4, 1962, asks, "Was this a coincidence?" referring to the guilt she felt at losing a child near to being born. She seemed to abandon all possibility of children through her abortions.

Haspiel writes that on July 17, 1960 Marilyn went to the airport to fly to Hollywood to appear in *The Misfits*. He walked up to her as she was about to board the plane. She turned to him and, he said, "I took one look at her ravaged face and refused to accept what my eyes could see so clearly. I turned away from her. I literally turned away from her!" He noticed as she ran to board the plane that "there were several menstrual stains visible on the lower half of the back of her beige skirt...I knew that she had extremely painful periods, so she had obviously had a very bad night...She looked awful and, emotionally speaking, I just needed to reject this image of her on the spot."

After she divorced Miller on January 20, 1961, eleven nights later she attended a sneak preview of *The Misfits* at the Capitol Theater on Broadway. It opened on February 1, 1961 and Haspiel recalls, "The day after I saw the film, its newly divorced star entered the Payne Whitney Psychiatric Clinic and shortly went from there over to the Columbia Presbyterian Centre on the upper west side." He adds that he was told she took twenty sleeping pills a night at times, "enough to destroy the average person."

Six months later Marilyn was ready to leave New York for Los Angeles when she suddenly was forced to have the gall bladder operation, then set out for the West coast. Haspiel cites an incident which, he believes, became Marilyn's "real and ultimate motivation for departing New York City to an atmosphere that suddenly appeared a safety zone."

He says Paula Strasberg, "Marilyn's like-family personal friend and acting coach told me this sad story, advising me that the only people who knew anything about this event were Marilyn, Marilyn's psychiatrist, Paula and her husband Lee."

An actress, who remains anonymous, requested Marilyn to help her understand "a scene I am preparing to do at the Actors Studio." Marilyn accepted the woman's invitation to lunch after she explained that she wanted to go over the scene "to see if you maybe can help me out with what should be my motivation here, my inner feelings."

They were seated in a booth as the woman plied Marilyn with drinks, then led her into the lines of a scripted love scene. Suddenly the actress embraced Marilyn in an obvious "male-to-female way, then kissed her directly and passionately on the lips!" Haspiel reported. The woman also "attempted to enter Marilyn's mouth with her tongue." She had arranged for reporters to be seated nearby to observe her in what would appear a lesbian embrace with Marilyn in a public place. Marilyn, shocked, at once realized something was wrong, rose from the table and rushed out of the restaurant.

Haspiel says the incident became Marilyn's reason for leaving New York at once "for an atmosphere that suddenly looked as something of a safety zone to her." This incident may have also prompted Marilyn to start at once the five-times-a-week sessions with Dr. Greenson.

Haspiel last saw Marilyn at 4 A.M. on "the now immortal night of May 19, 1962 when Marilyn sang 'Happy Birthday' to President Kennedy at the old Madison Square Garden on Eighth Avenue and 50th Street." Haspiel described meeting Marilyn at her apartment at an early morning hour when she returned home, "not knowing this would be our last time together." He said her face was "incredibly beautiful, movingly vulnerable. Her hair looked like white spun gold, eyes descended to the rhinestone-like gems sewn onto her dazzling gown, now eliciting flickers of light, those beams bouncing off the flesh-tone material encasing her magnificent body."

She would be dead two and a half months later.

Psychoanalysts believe any woman who chooses sexual contact with as many men as Marilyn did, is unconsciously trying to gain possession of the powerful penis. The act of sex momentarily provides such women with this illusionary wish as the man's power ebbs for the moment.

The wish for sex appeared in the parts Marilyn played in her twenty-nine completed films. In her private life no one but she knew how many men she was sexually involved with for an hour, a few weeks, perhaps months. She seemed to act out of a childish wantonness, whether it was the sex she at first offered men to further her career or the sex she indulged in after she was famous. There appears little difference between having a cup of coffee, a Coca Cola or sex in the film world of Hollywood, as Dr. Martin Grotjahn, a well-known psychoanalyst, once observed.

Some men sought Marilyn so they could boast they had gone to bed with the world's sex symbol. Marilyn once told a photographer who asked for a sexual liaison, "Zip up your fly and get back to the camera. I never have to do that again. I'm a star." At last she felt she could be more discriminating, choose carefully the men about whom she felt passionate for the moment.

In talking of her first marriage to Jim Dougherty on June 19, 1942, right after Marilyn turned sixteen, she said, "It wasn't love. It was to get a place of my own. I *wanted* to be an actress; I've always wanted that—as far back as I can remember I was always day- dreaming."

As a little girl she yearned with all her heart to appear one day on the movie screen. To be an actress meant she could for a while blot out the cruel world, live in the make-believe of the written word. Pretend she was falling in love, marrying. Or, as in *Niagara*, plotting the death of a husband so she could marry another man with whom she had fallen in love after her husband returned from a mental hospital.

Marilyn said further of her marriage to Dougherty, "Mrs. Dougherty," meaning herself, "was a different person; it was Norma Jean which was my name then. You can say that any one person is many people. Norma Jean is still alive inside me but in quite a different way."

There were a number of reasons she became an actress. The name her mother gave her, Norma, was one of them. Norma Talmadge was described by David Thomson in *Film Biography* as the oldest of the three Talmadge sisters and the most successful until "sound proved the incongruity of salon prettiness and tenement voice and made *DuBarry, Woman of Paris*, her last film. Only thirty-three, she had been in the movies since 1911 and was one of the most popular of silent screen actresses, animated, able to play romance and comedy."

Thomson also calls Norma Talmadge "a natural-born comic; you could turn on a scene with her and she'd go on for five minutes without stopping or repeating herself." Perhaps Marilyn absorbed some of her sense of the comic from seeing many Talmadge silent movies with her mother on the precious Saturdays her mother visited her at the foster home.

Norma married Joseph Schenck, then formed the Norma Talmadge Production Company with Schenck as supervisor of the majority of her films. Marilyn would also later form her own company, as though copying Norma.

Norma called Schenck "Daddy" as Marilyn did her husbands. In the early 1920s Schenck used his wife's box-office power to buy himself into United Artists, Thomson said. The Schencks were divorced in 1930 when Marilyn was four years old. Thomson reports, "Norma took her maligned voice into radio and later married George Jessel but she never made another film." She died in 1957, "a hopeless drug addict," according to Guiles. Did Marilyn consciously or unconsciously end her life as her first film idol did?

Another man who wrote briefly of his experiences with Marilyn as she slowly started her career climb was Elia Kazan, with whom she had an affair. First an actor, then a famous director on Broadway, following this in Hollywood, and recently author of his eloquent autobiography, *A Life*, Kazan arrived in the City of Angels in early January, 1951.

He carried with him an original screen play *The Hook* by Arthur Miller, hoping to direct it for Darryl Zanuck, head of Marilyn's production company, Twentieth Century-Fox. Kazan later directed the films *Gentleman's Agreement*, *A Tree Grows in Brooklyn*, *On the Waterfront*, *East of Eden* and *Baby Doll*, among others.

One day Kazan stood on a set where his friend Harmon Jones, the director, suddenly wanted the actors onstage. Kazan heard Jones call out, "Marilyn." Then, in brusquer tone, "Marilyn!"

She still did not appear. Jones said to Kazan, "That girl drives me nuts." Kazan asked, "What's the matter with her?"

Jones replied, "She can't stop crying. All right, the man who was keeping her died, but that was three weeks ago. Every time I need her, she's in the next stage, crying. It puffs up her eyes."

Kazan had seen Marilyn two months before while dining at Chasen's with Abe Lastfogel, a partner in the famed William Morris Agency. Sitting at the same table was Abe's powerful associate, Johnny Hyde, one of the leading agents in Hollywood, vice-president of the William Morris Agency. His "devoted companion," as Kazan put it, "was a fair-haired young woman, not blond, not straw, not platinum as she would later be, but a lovely natural light brown."

He described her further as having the classic beauty of the all-American small-town girl. When she looked at Johnny she gave him "that dazed starlet look of unqualified adoration and utter dependence." Kazan had been introduced to her but did not catch her name.

Now when Marilyn appeared on the set Kazan asked Jones to introduce him. He invited her to dinner but she declined, sorrow in her voice, still obviously mourning the man she described as "the architect of her career." Hyde, whose clients included Lana Turner and Rita Hayworth, had fallen desperately in love with Marilyn, who was twenty-one compared to his fifty-three. He pleaded with her to marry him, she told him she loved him but was "not in love with" him. Nevertheless he left his wife and three sons, bought a large home on North Palm Drive, asked Marilyn to live with him. She kept her apartment but spent many nights at his house.

One day Hyde took her to the Thalberg Building to read for John Huston and a possible part in the film *The Asphalt Jungle*. Huston then chose her to play Angela, the blond mistress of Louis Calhern, one of the famous crooks. Huston thus became the director of Marilyn's first important film, one that started her on the road to fame. He also would be director of her final film, *The Misfits*.

He later said of Marilyn, as quoted in *The Hustons* by Lawrence Grobel, "She moved women as much as she did men, it wasn't just a sex thing, that was no more than half of her attraction." He added that the other half included her spirit of courage, her humor, her vulnerability as a woman, which he said she displayed to perfection in her two scenes in *The Asphalt Jungle*. Her career was launched when he accepted her for this small role and she remained forever grateful, called him the first genius she had met.

Hyde introduced her to Ben Lyons, former film star, then the head of casting for Fox Studios. He told her she would have to change her name from Norma Jean Dougherty to a more seductive one. He proposed "Marilyn Miller" after the famous Broadway singing and dancing star of several decades earlier. Norma Jean then suggested that her grandmother's last name by her first husband, "Monroe," be the second part of her new name, accepting "Marilyn" as the first part. She carried with her from then on a daily reminder of the grandmother who, when Norma Jean was nineteen months old, had gone insane and died nineteen days later.

Marilyn wrote Lyons, with whom it was said she had a brief affair, "You found me, named me and believed in me when no one else did. My love and thanks forever."

Before Hyde appeared in her life, Marilyn had been courted by Joseph Schenck, then one of the richest and most respected men in the film community. Marilyn told Kazan that Schenck, at seventy-one, had proposed to her. She added he pointed out he was "not long for this world" and she, as his widow, would inherit sixty million dollars. As she did with Hyde, she refused to accept his proposal. It was not money she wanted but fame in the films.

Two weeks before Christmas, 1950, Marilyn was living in Hyde's mansion, recovering from surgery on her nose, preparing to appear in new films Hyde had arranged. The fleshy tip of her nose had made it look too long for the screen so it was lifted a notch. This gave her more upper lip between nose and lips so her smile was wider, more seductive. Cartilage was also placed in her jaw to make her chin line stronger. Parts of Marilyn's face and her new name were strangers to Norma Jean.

At this time Hyde, whose heart had troubled him for years, began to lose weight at a dangerous rate. He complained of shortness of breath. He suffered a fatal heart attack on December 15. Marilyn remained by his side that final night in Cedars of Lebanon Hospital, the only time that we know of she saw anyone die.

After attending his funeral she left the house on North Palm Drive, now claimed by his family, to stay overnight with her coach, Natasha Lytess. It was then Marilyn made her first suicide attempt.

Natasha later reported that as she opened the door to the room Marilyn occupied she saw Marilyn lying limp on the bed. Natasha shook her by the shoulders but there was no response. Then she saw "an ooze of purple paste in the lip-corners and forced my fingers into her mouth...It was crammed full of this purplish paste—there must have been about thirty Nembutal capsules wadded in her mouth. Enough to kill five people."

Marilyn had not swallowed them, she later explained, because her throat had dried up in terror as she put the pills in her mouth. Natasha said Marilyn had been lying there, waiting for the pills to melt and trickle down, destroy her life. Natasha commented, "She hadn't expected me back for hours."

This was the first of her many attempts at suicide. One of the undercurrents in the suicidal soul is a deep feeling of guilt. Marilyn no doubt felt guilty because she had stolen Hyde from his wife and sons and somehow felt she had caused his death.

The year before she met Hyde she had fallen desperately in love with Fred Karger, her vocal coach, who had recently divorced. She called him her "first love." He introduced her to literature and classical music, taught her how to sing for the films. She wanted to marry him but he did not believe she would be the kind of wife he wished. He later married Jane Wyman after she divorced Ronald Reagan. Karger and Wyman were eventually divorced, then remarried.

Karger's rejection of Marilyn no doubt revived the earlier most traumatic rejections of her life—by her father and later, her mother. From then on it seemed as though she unconsciously decided she would be the one to do the rejecting. She started with her first husband, Dougherty, when he returned from the South Pacific.

Though turned down the first time Kazan asked Marilyn to dine with him, he had a second chance when they met not long after in a cafeteria. This time, having more fully mourned Hyde's death, Marilyn accepted Kazan's invitation to dinner. He described her as having "little education and no knowledge except of her own experience."

He added, "For an actor that is the important kind of knowledge." He also commented, "She found everything either completely meaningless or completely personal. She had no interest in abstract, formal or impersonal concepts but was passionately devoted to her life experience."

What Marilyn needed most of all, he said, "was to have her sense of worth affirmed. Born out of wedlock, abandoned by her parents, kicked around, scorned by the men she'd been with until Johnny, she wanted more than anything else approval from men she could respect. Comparing her with many of the wives I got to know in that community, I thought her the honest one, them the 'chumps'."

He noted what he called "one fatal contradiction" in Marilyn. She desperately sought reassurance of her worth yet respected those who scorned her "because their estimate of her was her own." This was how she felt as a child whose mother and father did not think enough of her as a human being to take care of her, help her cope with some people's contempt of her ability to act, even though both her sexiness and comic wit shone in every film.

When Kazan started his affair with Marilyn, she lived in a small apartment near Natasha, who was giving her lessons "on the cuff." Kazan describes Marilyn's dwelling as consisting of one large room, empty except for a white concert piano Kazan never heard her play but knew "this large instrument meant something special to her." It was the piano her mother bought for the house where she and Norma Jean finally lived together for three months, until Gladys was taken away in a strait-jacket, screaming, to the mental hospital. The piano had been sold along with the rest of the furniture. After Marilyn earned enough money years later she went on a search for it, found it at an auction.

Kazan listened to her stories about her life, said at times she would weep and he would comfort her. He described her as having "a bomb inside her. Ignite her and she exploded. Her lover was her savior." Sometimes they spent the night at a friend of Kazan's named Charles Feldman, who had been head of Famous Artists, an agency that represented Marilyn for a time, before he became an eminent producer.

One night Feldman gave a party for Arthur Miller, who had won the Pulitzer Prize for his play *Death of a Salesman*. Kazan was supposed to pick up Marilyn but first had to interview an actress Zanuck urged him to consider for *Zepata*, which Kazan wanted to direct.

Incidentally, Zanuck later became Marilyn's *bête noire* in that he continued to keep her salary unconscionably low. Kazan, in his book

A Life, believes Marilyn's greatest appeal for men was not her physical beauty but the "rescue fantasy" she inspired in men who wanted somehow to help her feel fulfilled and "saved" from whatever demons drove her.

On the night of the party Kazan phoned Miller, asked him to pick up Marilyn whom Miller had never met, at her apartment and explain that Kazan would meet them at the party after he interviewed the actress. Miller phoned Marilyn, introduced himself, said he would call for her. She protested that she would take a taxi, meet him at the Feldman home at the appropriate time. Miller insisted she be escorted by him. According to Kazan, the first thing that impressed Marilyn about her future husband was that he refused to allow her to go to a party alone in a taxi. Kazan added he thought, "How little these glamour girls expect of life."

When Kazan finished his meeting with the actress he drove to Feldman's house. There he found Marilyn and Miller dancing "and the lovely light of desire was in their eyes." He described Miller as a good dancer, "tall and handsome in a Lincolnesque way." Marilyn seemed happy in his arms, "all her doubts about her worth were being satisfied in one package." Miller at this time was married, had two children.

After the party thinned out, the three sat on a sofa, talked a while, then Kazan said he was tired, asked Miller to take Marilyn home. From then on, from time to time, Kazan said he continued to see her but sensed "she had a violent crush on Arthur" because she did not speak of much else.

He observed that, like himself, Marilyn "always felt in danger. She never felt sure of herself, who she was." Even as a success she lacked self-esteem, feared authority, could not accept praise because her faith in herself was so low.

❦ ❦ ❦

Dr. Greenson told a colleague that the Miller marriage had collapsed "to a considerable degree" on sexual grounds. He said Marilyn believed she was frigid, "found it difficult to sustain a series of orgasms with the same individual." This could be attributed to the guilt that followed her fantasy that each man was her elusive father. To have sex with one's father is forbidden, a sign of "craziness." The fantasy often remains, however, it may become the eternal plight of a woman who emotionally still remains a child seeking in vain to work through the oedipal rivalry, a natural part of maturing.

Marilyn was never able to face this fantasy. She was driven from one sexual encounter to the next, believing it love, only to find it ending in fear and hatred from which she fled. Such consuming sexual need is called the Casanova complex, named after the man whose promiscuity became famous. The aftermath of the sudden hatred that shortly appears in promiscuous relationships is caused by the excessive guilt that becomes pervasive at the unconscious realization the sexual partner is the mother (for the man) or the father (for the woman) desired in childhood.

The Don Juan, masculine or feminine, never knows the love that is "a many-splendored thing," that includes respect for the self and for the parents of childhood, knowing they did the best they could in terms of their childhood. If such understanding occurs, love and respect for the marital partner exists, along with the awareness that neither can be perfect.

Love is one thing, passion another. Passion ensures the continuation of the human race even though the passion does not last, often destroyed by the demands each makes upon the other as the faults of both emerge.

Sexual desire also represents in fantasy the embracing arms and giving breast of a mother, feelings that precede the oedipal wish. When Marilyn told a friend, as she married Arthur Miller, "Now I won't have to suck cock any more," she referred to a sexual practice more akin to feeding at the breast than expression of mature love. She unconsciously also thought of a man as a substitute mother, wanted him to grant her every wish, especially sexual—in all its stages from infancy to adulthood.

When Marilyn was a novice she used sex to get parts in films. She is reported to have said that for a very brief time at the start of her career she had even been a call girl. She saw sex, as many women do, not only as a way of unconsciously still trying to get a mother's love but for the release of a hidden rage. She unconsciously sought to be rejected by a man, re-enacting that which had been done unto her.

Marilyn was not capable of a love that held trust, respect, tolerance for the other person's faults. She wished to be perfect, another fantasy of childhood, and in turn expected the man to be perfect.

But in spite of her tragic childhood she showed tremendous strengths. She refused to allow a man to keep her, as several offered to do, even in splendor. She rose to the top of the movie kingdom after many initial turndowns. She tried to overcome the past for the most part of thirty-six years. Then it exploded with a vengeance.

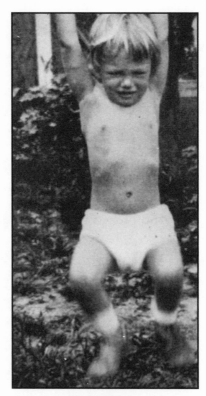

**Norma Jean
cheesecake at age 3**
© Robert F. Slatzer

3.
Of Murder Concealed

Marilyn's sweetness was a mammoth mask, one she discarded in the presence of those few people she trusted. On screen she appeared like "some sweet kid," as Louis Calhern kept referring to her when she played his youthful mistress in *The Asphalt Jungle*. But underneath the "sweet kid" disguise raged a forlorn little girl.

Marilyn said she made others believe in something she knew was wrong, then discovered she could deceive herself, too, momentarily believe the "vital lie" she played out in front of them. The price she paid, as we all do when we are unable to face the truth about our feelings, was the highest. She could not sleep, took too many pills, too much alcohol, broke down and had to start from the beginning again, never able "to get out of this vicious circle," as she told Lembourn.

Part of the "vital lie" was her seduction of others, promising them love when she knew she would soon detest them. Such seduction was part of her every move and, no doubt, a large portion of her personal life.

She had attempted numerous suicides, starting with Johnny Hyde's death. Everyone who commits suicide, or tries to, or thinks about doing so, whether aware of it or not, hides a violent rage in his heart. He wishes to murder someone who has hurt him deeply but instead turns the fury on himself, as Marilyn did. It reached the point of no return when life itself finally became too tormenting to endure.

The male murderer in the popular television film *Double-Take* tells Richard Crenna, who plays the detective, that the act of murder "is not enough." The person who commits suicide feels deeper satisfaction before he dies than the one who murders, according to Dr. Herbert S. Strean, psychoanalyst and author of *Our Wish to Kill, The Murder in All Our Hearts*.

In turning murderous wishes on herself rather than kill those who emotionally wounded her, Marilyn believed she thus took revenge. On the surface her suicide seemed revenge on her alleged last lover, Robert Kennedy, for promising to marry her, then changing his mind, making her feel once again unwanted and unloved.

"The suicidal person takes pleasure in the thought others will suffer, feel guilty, blame themselves for the death," Dr. Strean explains. "This is true of sons and daughters whose parents have hurt them, as well as those lovers who kill themselves when a supposed sweetheart rejects them. The adolescent or adult who murders himself is saying, 'I won't kill the one I love and need desperately but I'll kill myself and then he will feel sorry the rest of his life because he was so cruel to me.'"

Marilyn also felt like a murderer after each abortion. Eventually she had her Fallopian tubes tied, later untied when she wanted a child with Miller. Then all she could manage to produce were two miscarriages, which made her feel desperate, not woman enough to produce a baby. Once again a failure.

Following the deaths of both Hyde and Gable, her lover in *The Misfits*, Marilyn felt suicidal. What made her feel so guilty, think of herself as a murderer in each instance?

Her guilt arose from the fantasy that she caused the man to die. Both were older men and in her unconscious they represented her father. She told Gable he looked like her real father, whose photograph her mother showed her as a child. He was the man she hoped to get even with one day because he had denied she was his daughter, refused to marry Gladys, made Norma Jean feel she was not important enough to warrant the love of a father.

Marilyn hid within herself a titanic rage from her first awareness of her father's rejection until the day she died. She felt worthless, hated by everyone. At times she claimed to love the world but she loved no one man or woman, daily battled an inner fury.

As a child she had desperately wanted a full-time mother and this she also lacked. She was fortunate if she saw Gladys on Saturday afternoons when she traveled from her apartment by trolley to the foster home where Marilyn spent her first eight years. Though she did not express it, she would have to feel a rage at her mother for deserting her the rest of the week, again to feel unwanted, alone in the universe.

In her four-year marriage to Dougherty, Marilyn never showed an iota of anger, according to Guiles who interviewed Dougherty at length. Guiles writes of Marilyn's later "flashes of rage or periods of cool disdain." He adds that her sudden shifts in mood resulted in the breakup of several relationships of long standing. These included her first dramatic coach, Natasha Lytess, to whom Marilyn was close for seven years, as well as Miller and Dougherty.

But with many other men in her brief life she repeated what her parents had done to her—complete abandonment. Our parents are our role models as we grow up. We consciously and unconsciously copy their acts, attitudes, philosophy of life.

Marilyn's shortest relationship in marriage was to Robert Slatzer, a writer, who first saw her in the summer of 1946 when she was an aspiring actress, just about to sign her first studio contract. He dated her for the next few years during her ascent to stardom. According to him, their secret wedding took place on October 4, 1952, in Tijuana, Mexico, ended three days later.

Zanuck called Marilyn into his office after learning of the marriage, told her he had spent thousands of dollars on her upcoming career, suggested strongly she at once undo the marriage. Marilyn and Slatzer returned to Tijuana, located the attorney who married them, he destroyed the wedding license. They remained friends over the years except for the DiMaggio era when the baseball star forbade Marilyn to see any of her former men friends. She stood this sanction for nine months, then decided to divorce him when he wanted her to give up acting.

Marilyn wrote she had once wanted to express anger at Zanuck when Twentieth Century-Fox did not pick up her second option at the start of her career. For her a difficult act, she marched to his office to tell him how she felt. She was informed by a secretary he was out of town. Marilyn then was furious at herself, Guiles reports, and decided any girl who sought to know why she was unwanted only asked for "another grievous wound to her ego." Guiles describes Marilyn as "wholly dedicated to herself, unable to relate to others in any real way, without any steadying support for her ego." We all need strong supports if we wish to come to terms with the inevitable frustrations and pains. We can never achieve all we wish, frustration is part of living with those who differ from us in smaller or larger measure. Without the support of others, life turns grim, sad, hopeless.

With the release of *The Asphalt Jungle*, even though she played only a small part, she was on her way to fame. Her voice, body and sense of humor became unforgettable. As a result of a rush of work in 1949 and 1950, she had six films released in one year, four set up by agent-lover Hyde.

But slowly the frustrations set in and her way of dealing with anger, evident throughout her film career, was to "sleep it off," after drinking heavily. She claimed alcohol alone was not enough to put her to sleep, she needed the follow-up pills that quickly allowed her to drift off to the hidden valleys of the unconscious mind.

Guiles also describes her as "insecure, hypersensitive and mistrusting of others." Above all, she could not tolerate rejection, it drove her to a feeling of desperation.

She suffered a severe rejection as her third Twentieth Century-Fox film, *Let's Make It Legal*, was edited in the fall of 1951. She now felt just enough pride in herself to decide, at the age of twenty- five, that she wanted to meet the man she believed to be her real father. She discovered C. Stanley Gifford had bought the Red Rock Dairy Farm outside Hemet, a rural village near Palm Springs.

She phoned Natasha, asked if she would drive to Hemet with her. She said, "I'm going to see my father at his farm and talk to him."

Just before they reached the farm, Marilyn stopped the car at a highway telephone booth, told her drama coach, "I'm going to phone him. I can't just barge in on him this way." According to Guiles to whom one of Marilyn's "trusted confidantes" told the story, Marilyn asked the woman who answered the phone, "Is Mr. Gifford there?"

"Who's calling?" the woman inquired.

"This is Marilyn. I'm his child. I mean, the little girl years ago, Gladys Baker's daughter. He's sure to know who I am," she said in that soft, seductive voice.

The woman said, "I don't know who you are but I'll tell him you're on the phone."

Marilyn waited, in a few moments heard the woman say, "He doesn't want to see you. He suggests you see his lawyer in Los Angeles if you have some complaint. Do you have a pencil?"

"No," she said. "I don't have a pencil." Then, "Goodbye," hung up.

At that moment she must have felt utterly alone in the world. Defeated, rejected once more by the man who had in part created her. Though at least she now knew his name and he was acknowledging her, even if only to say, "See my lawyer."

Her rage over her inability to meet with Gifford and get him to admit she was his daughter that day she drove to Hemet, had to be violent. She would hate him inexorably until the day she died, wish him dead many times for causing her so much grief and mourning. Both for not acknowledging her as his daughter—he could have married her mother then quickly divorced her so his child would at least have had a last name to ensure her respectability in a world that did not approve of "bastards"—and for the latest rejection as she humbled herself to seek him out.

She later felt a sense of revenge when, at the height of her fame Gifford called one day from a hospital, relaying a message through his nurse. The nurse explained to Marilyn that her father might be dying and wished to see her. Remembering his answer of a few years back, still suffering the emotional scars, Marilyn said coolly, "Tell him he can call my lawyer," and hung up. Gifford lived on but they never met. She could not forgive his earlier slight, one that cut to the heart. She must have ached to be the nemesis in his life, to now cut him down as he had cut her off at birth.

With the groundwork laid by Hyde, Marilyn's career soared. During her contract with Twentieth Century-Fox, she was given sixteen film roles, including *Bus Stop*, *The Seven Year Itch* and *Gentlemen Prefer Blondes*. The first movie by the Marilyn Monroe Productions enterprise, managed by Milton Greene, a former photographer, was *The Prince and the Showgirl*. It was filmed in London and starred Sir Lawrence Olivier, England's leading actor, also the director.

At this time Marilyn became known for what Guiles calls her "notorious unpunctuality." It was no accident this occurred when she felt deep rejection by two men—her new husband and Olivier.

Just after her marriage, she and Miller had set out for London. Marilyn would later tell Lena Pepitone, "I think Olivier hated me. He gave me the dirtiest looks, even when he was smiling. I was sick half the time but he didn't believe me, or else he didn't care. He looked at me like he had just smelled a pile of dead fish. Like I was a leper or something as awful. I felt like a little fool the whole time."

Then came a far deeper hurt. One day Marilyn noticed an entry in Miller's daily notebook, which he had left on his desk open to the most recent observations. As though he wanted her to read it, perhaps unconsciously hoping she would change.

As she told the Strasbergs, who were in England at the time, "It was something about how disappointed he was in me. That his first wife had let him down but I had done something worse. That Olivier was beginning to think I was a troublesome bitch and that he, Arthur, no longer had a decent answer to that one."

She later said he had written the following about her in his notebook: "Why do you like to hurt me if you love me? I thought you were an angel but Mary [his first wife] was a saint compared to you. Olivier is right. You are a troublesome bitch. What a waste of love! All you want is a flunky. Someone who'll make excuses for you, wait on you night and day, pour out sweet talk to make you feel better and wake you up from the stupor of pills. Well, I'm not up to it...The only one I really love in this world is my daughter."

He said the same thing, though not in these words, when he later wrote *After the Fall*. Part of this play painted a devastating portrait of Marilyn, whom he named Maggie. The leading man, Quentin, obviously Miller, tells Maggie, his wife, "We used one another!" And then, "You eat those pills to blind yourself, but if you could only say 'I have been cruel,' this frightening room would open. If you could say 'I have been kicked around, but I have been just as inexcusably vicious to others, called my husband an idiot in public. I have been utterly selfish despite my generosity. I have been hurt by a long line of men but I have cooperated with my persecutors.'"

Her cooperation was not a conscious one. She was driven by unconscious wishes of such magnitude that no one could fulfill them. She was filled with hate, always accompanied by the death wish for the hated one. At the same time, as in childhood, she did not openly dare defy her "persecutors."

Marilyn was now in such an emotional state that Paula Strasberg called Marilyn's analyst in New York, Dr. Kris and convinced her to fly to London to calm Marilyn down. After a few sessions with Dr. Kris, Marilyn was able to finish the film. She would never forget Miller's notebook blow but she tried to make the marriage work, remained with him for four years.

Whitey Snyder, her make-up man from the start of her career until the day she died, told Guiles, "The trouble with Marilyn was she didn't trust her own judgment, always had someone around to depend on. Coaches, so-called friends. Even me."

Trust is the basis of love, she allowed nobody to trust her and she really never trusted anyone else. This would also include her psychoanalyst, at first, for it takes time, sometimes months, perhaps years, before a patient trusts his analyst. In fantasy, the analyst is first seen as the untrustworthy parent of childhood.

When Guiles interviewed Miller he said, "Marilyn had this fear of involvement which would endanger her personally. People in her situation are either victims or else they're the aggressor—which they can't bear the thought of."

Marilyn was both—the victim and the aggressor. In most instances she was afraid to be the aggressor. Instead, she turned her murderous wishes on herself, over and over, until they finally exploded on August 4, 1962 in a final fury. The suicide murders the self but also in fantasy the hated person who has been psychically taken within so that he becomes a part of the hidden self for whom the victim writes scripts of passion and revenge.

In his recent autobiography *Timebends* Arthur Miller describes Marilyn as "the saddest girl I've ever known...a woman on the knife edge of self-destruction all her adult life." He also might have added, "and all her early life, too, from the day she opened her eyes to the hurtful world."

If Marilyn had been able to know the depths of her fury, accept she was entitled to feel it because she lacked a father and most of the time a mother as well when she grew up, she might have sought therapy much earlier and lived many more years in comparative acceptance of herself. But the "ifs" do not help us—we have to understand why we felt enraged and understand, too, that our parents, out of their own frailties, could not give any more than they did.

Miller described Marilyn as living in a "swamp of doubt" and unbelievably vulnerable, desperate for reassurance. She only believed she was loved during the act of sex, as Miller portrayed so movingly in the character of the wife in *After the Fall*. He also wrote Marilyn was so "vivid" in her screen performances that she did not disappear after death. This is proved by the many people all over the world who still wish to read about her or constantly watch her films.

Her ability to genuinely portray both a real and a comic sense on screen, as few actresses have been capable of doing, has kept her alive. Her performances always seem fresh, new, believable, which is why we are able to see her films over and over. We are never bored but enjoy them, finding new dimensions each time we watch her, hear her seductive, often laughing voice.

🐛 🐛 🐛

Living with Miller eventually brought out some of the buried fury Marilyn had managed fairly well to hide up to then. This was graphically described by Lena Pepitone as they spent day after day on the thirteenth floor of 44 East 57th Street in the apartment where Marilyn and Miller lived. It was one of the few apartment houses in the city to offer a thirteenth floor, for the majority of owners believed the number "13" unlucky. Though it proved to be so for Marilyn, the causes were far deeper, much more complex than the number of the apartment floor.

Describing the years she worked for Marilyn as the most interesting and rewarding of her life, Lena wrote in *Marilyn Monroe, Confidential*, with William Stadiem, "As I came to know her, I saw what a remarkable woman she really was. Yes, she did have problems— strange habits, crazy moods and intense frustrations most people just don't have to deal with. But she also had a good heart, a terrific sense of humor and the kindest understanding of other people's troubles. She understood all about troubles because she had had so many—too many—of her own."

Lena, Marilyn's wardrobe mistress and personal maid, observed that Miller kept himself closeted in his workroom most of the day and even during the evenings after supper. May Reis, Marilyn's private secretary, manager of the household, was also present during the weekdays. Marilyn went out only for two purposes—to attend sessions at the Actors Studio and to see Dr. Kris, recommended by the Strasbergs.

Lena was astounded by Marilyn's drinking habits—a Bloody Mary on arising, usually late morning, followed by a glass of champagne, then breakfast. She seemed to need the stimulation of alcohol to get through the day at this stage of her life. Lena was also amazed at Marilyn's walking around nude, as though this were the custom. She never wore underwear, claimed, "It's so uncomfortable."

Lembourne wrote he believed Marilyn "was happiest when she's naked...Naked, she discovered whatever was most genuine in herself." Before she became a success she posed nude for the calendar that later became famous. It never fazed her to appear nude in front of anyone. She recalled that when she was a little girl and went to church, as the organ played and everyone sang, "then the impulse would come to me to take off all my clothes. I wanted desperately to stand up naked for God and everyone else to see. I had to clench my teeth and sit on my hands to keep myself from undressing. Sometimes I had to pray hard and beg God to keep me from taking my clothes off."

She added, "My impulse to appear naked and my dreams about it had no shame or sense of sin. Dreaming of people looking at me made me feel less lonely."

To appear nude made her "feel less lonely," less the abandoned little girl whom no one looked at except perhaps when she would wander all around the house nude and was told to get dressed at once so the other foster children would not see her naked. Or perhaps the only time her mother touched her was when she bathed her little daughter on a Saturday afternoon visit, and this was when Norma Jean felt most loved.

She was known in later life for walking stark naked into a room of her house in front of people, not caring what they thought. This is the innocent child appearing without clothes in front of his parents, an acting-out of a normal desire of early childhood.

She also felt comfortable appearing naked among wardrobe women, makeup girls, hairdressers. "Being naked seems to soothe her— almost hypnotize her," Natasha said. Marilyn told a director who ordered her to wear panties under her dress, "Pants gag me."

Over the years she kept in touch with David Conover, the photographer who first discovered her. According to Conover in *Finding Marilyn: A Romance*, she was "proud of her body and loved to show it off." It was the one part of her about which she always felt confident. Her lovely body was her only security.

Conover told her he thought the reason some people found her difficult to understand was because she appeared "so changeable." She admitted, "Sometimes I find I have more than two sides. I am so many different persons. I definitely change, with places as well as with people. In fact, I feel that I'm always in a state of change."

She said, "It's funny. I've got so many selves I wish I knew which one was me. It was confusing at first until I found that some of my friends were that way too. Frankie [Frank Sinatra] carries around with him a dozen different people. You're the only person I know who is always the same," addressing Conover.

Conover asked if she worried about death, if it bothered her at times. She replied, "I'm afraid of death. But not as much as I am of old age." Which, to her, meant going insane, like her mother and grandmother.

Then he asked if she ever thought of suicide. She shook her head "no," added, "not deliberately. Once or twice I've taken an overdose of sleeping pills. But only accidentally. With Nembutals, you never know when you've had one too many." As though she were playing Russian roulette with pills. She added that she believed everyone at times had thought about suicide.

When Conover praised her for not having lost the "sweetness of Norma Jean," she laughed again, said, "I can't seem to shake her. Even if I wanted to. She's my alter ego—very sensitive and easily hurt. Every time someone takes advantage of Norma Jean, I become a real bitch." She looked into Conover's eyes, asked, "You've never seen my bitchy side, have you?" He replied, "No. Not really."

Marilyn was saying she could not shake the hurt of childhood, that its torment was easily aroused. And that now she was the powerful Marilyn Monroe, she could afford to be a "bitch" whenever she felt offended, either by top studio executive or husband.

Before he left, Conover asked how she liked living alone in Brentwood, where she had just bought a house. She said, "The worst problem is at night. That's when I hate being alone. Maybe I should get married again. What makes the day really worthwhile is having someone to curl up with at night...I have to take a lot more sleeping pills. They do help, but not as much as having a man around."

Here Marilyn was describing sex as a soporific—a man in her bed helped her forget the pain of the world more easily than consuming sleeping pills. Also preferable to the pills was inherent in the question she next asked Conover, "Do you believe masturbating is harmful?"

He said he thought it a natural way to let off pressure. She looked relieved, he noted.

They were both, as he put it, "very sloshed" by that time and other people drinking in the Barbizon Plaza's cocktail lounge stared at them curiously. She then asked if he had ever masturbated and he admitted he did. Then she looked "mischievous," suggested they "should get together, it would solve both their problems." He laughed but did not take her up on it. He told her that if he ever had sex with her he was afraid he could never leave her. Implying this would be his destruction, knowing she could not be faithful to him.

Marilyn was telling him that in spite of all the sex she had enjoyed, was still enjoying, she sometimes masturbated, which meant there was never enough sex. But more important, that sex represented not love for someone of the opposite sex but a hungry need still within herself, unsatisfied since childhood. A need from childhood, when masturbation was first enjoyed, a need that still persisted.

Lena described Marilyn at times like a Dr. Jekyll and Mr. Hyde when she had been drinking. One day Lena felt fear when Marilyn went into "a blind rage" after Lena ironed a blouse but failed to make the collar stiff enough. Marilyn hurled the blouse in Lena's face. Then instantly threw her arms around Lena, tears in her eyes, apologized like a sorry little girl who had defied her mother. Lena realized, she later wrote, that "patience was the only approach to Marilyn if one wanted to remain a friend."

She described Marilyn's life as "incredibly monotonous" except for her visits to Dr. Kris, who was trying to help her overcome her excessive need for alcohol and sleeping pills. Marilyn seemed to spend most of her time in her small bedroom, sleeping, looking at herself in the mirrors, drinking Bloody Marys and champagne and talking on the phone to DiMaggio, Sinatra or would-be producers, directors and stars who wanted to work with her. She also enjoyed playing jazz and blues records on the small machine next to her bed.

The song she played most often was "Every Day I Have the Blues," which included the words, "Nobody loves me, nobody seems to care." This mirrored her feelings about the world, myriad feelings that were intense when she was a tiny child living with foster parents. Marilyn often listened to Sinatra songs including "The Man I Love." Lena reported Marilyn would sing the words standing in front of a full-length picture of DiMaggio pasted inside her closet. Lena learned that after

Marilyn's divorce from DiMaggio in 1954, she lived for a while at Sinatra's house until she could find a place of her own as she and Frankie had a brief affair.

She openly showed her unhappiness and despair with Miller, hardly saw him during the day as he wrote away. He seldom wanted to leave the apartment at night, sometimes she wept in frustration when she expected to go out and he refused. She told Lena, "My life is shit. I can't go anywhere. I'm a prisoner in his house," fell weeping on the bed.

Though Marilyn was close to Lee and Paula Strasberg and their daughter Susan, and to the Norman Rostens, she felt she had no "real friends." She occasionally visited or invited to her apartment Miller's mother and father who seemed to genuinely like her. She called them at times "my family," her almost-real first family.

The once-deprived little girl, who rarely had new dresses, much less fabulously expensive ones, now shopped in the most luxurious department stores. She owned four mink coats, many velvet slacks, an array of sequined evening dresses with plunging necklines and "a large store" of flat Ferragamo shoes as well as high-heeled dressy pumps.

At times she feasted on steaks and lamb chops, with a side dish of cottage cheese. She loved Italian food, begged Lena, an expert at this, to prepare spaghetti, lasagna, sausages and peppers. She would belch and fart which, she soon learned, were signs of the malfunctioning gall bladder that had to be removed.

As Lena cleared Marilyn's small bedroom she would dust the pictures on the night stand by her bed. One was of a very attractive woman who, Marilyn explained was her mother, "lives in a sanitarium in California." At this point she was paying for her mother's care in the best private mental hospital she could find. The other photo was of Abraham Lincoln, she told Lena, laughing, "That's my father."

Then suddenly tears flooded her eyes and she sobbed, "Oh, Lena, I wish I had a father."

She often called her husbands "daddy," as though they were a replacement for her lost father, the man she needed most of all in her early life. Both father and mother are necessary for a child to mature successfully, the lack of one or the other produces deep unhappiness in the child, an unhappiness carried into adult years.

Lena concluded that Marilyn was almost always "sad" yet also almost always "sweet" in that she rarely took out her anger on her housekeeper and wardrobe mistress. She chiefly denigrated herself, at times would ask, "What the hell am I doing here? Is anything going to work out?"

She told Lena of her desire to act onstage and to find film scripts that did not portray her as "a dumb blonde." Added, "I've had enough of all that Hollywood shit."

She also told Lena, "I love being a star. After all I've been through, I won't quit now."

But her love of stardom was not strong enough to help her give up alcohol or sleeping pills. A star may shine and glitter in the public's image but may never be able to love herself enough to survive. Marilyn's denigration of herself ran deep, there were times her self-hatred reached new depths, chiefly after drinking.

One evening she called herself a "nobody," said to Lena, "What am I? Nothing. Look at me."

Lena reassured her, "Everybody loves you."

Marilyn stared at her, tears in her eyes, said, "It's all so crazy. If I only had someone to talk to." Miller as usual after dinner had retreated to his room to write.

"I did some bad things. Things that made me hate myself," Marilyn confessed. "Things *your* father kept you from doing."

She was no doubt referring to the many men with whom she had sex from her earliest modeling days to her marriage to Miller. She may have hoped that "making it" as a serious Broadway actress would wipe the slate clean of her guilt at using sex to climb the Hollywood ladder, act as pardon for the indiscriminate sleeping around that preceded her reaching the top.

She also recalled the only thing she really remembered of childhood was, "I was all by myself. All alone. For so long. I was a mistake. My mother didn't want to have me. She paid people to look after me.

I know I must have disgraced her. A divorced woman has enough problem in getting a man, I guess, but one with an illegitimate baby? I wish she had wanted me."

She felt unwanted not only by the father who never wished to see her but also by the mother who bore her and saw her as a rule once a week until Marilyn was eight. It was then that Gladys was taken to the mental hospital.

Lena said she was surprised that when Marilyn spoke of her father tears came to her eyes but not when she mentioned her mother. Once she asked, referring to her father, "Wouldn't he have even wanted to see what I was, how I turned out? Didn't he care at all?" No doubt thinking of the day she drove to his dairy farm and he refused to see her.

It became obvious to Lena and others in Marilyn's third year of marriage to Miller that she was now extremely unhappy. Lena thought him "a very distant husband," locked away in his room, writing, always writing. Marilyn would whisper, "Arthur's writing, he needs total quiet," if they talked too loudly.

Marilyn also said to Lena of Miller, "He makes me think I'm stupid, maybe I am stupid." This would make her feel again like the little girl in the foster home, then the orphanage, then more foster homes, about ten in all, until at sixteen she escaped by marrying Dougherty.

She wanted to get pregnant and finally did in the spring of 1957 but then had a miscarriage on August 1. Miller had been working for almost two years on a screenplay for Marilyn, based on his published short story, *The Misfits*. It had originally focused on several cowboys who wrangled wild horses to sell to dealers who took them to be slaughtered for dog food. Miller was accustomed, like most writers, to dedicating much of his time to whatever he worked on.

In all fairness to Miller, Marilyn's daily demands would seem impossible for any man to fulfill, as he portrayed it in *After the Fall*. She now became openly hostile to him, would not let Lena sew a button on one of his favorite sport shirts. She screamed at him, "Lena works for me! Not you." She said later to Lena, in extenuation of her outburst, "He won't do anything for me. He won't take me anyplace, let me have any fun. So I won't do anything for him." She seemed in a highly agitated state.

She was still demanding the fantasized "good father" and "good mother" she had never known. It was impossible for her, deprived so early in life of love and nurturing, to do anything but echo it over and over to anyone who would listen—the plea that someone, anyone, please meet all her emotional needs, still those of a child. She had little mature love to give, never having known what it meant to receive it.

Lena summed up what she believed Marilyn's feelings with the words, "She had become dissatisfied with almost every part of life." She and Miller seemed on the brink of splitting. She had suffered an earlier miscarriage, then an operation supposed to prevent a second miscarriage, but it did not, as she would soon find out.

She felt she was losing her shape, her body was getting old and flabby. Lena felt Dr. Kris did not seem to be helping Marilyn, for "every day Marilyn was either angry, hysterical or both." By now Lena cared very much for Marilyn, who seemed to cherish her, called her "Baby Lamb."

Marilyn had disbanded the Marilyn Monroe Productions, disenchanted with her co-owner Milton Greene. Then in 1958 Twentieth Century-Fox loaned her to Billy Wilder for a proposed movie. It centered on the story of two musicians who witness a gangland murder in Chicago and manage to flee the city dressed as women as they join Marilyn's all-girl band. It was titled *Some Like It Hot*. The film was made at the Sam Goldwyn Studios, home of United Artists.

Before long Marilyn became furious at the idea she would play the part of a girl so stupid she did not realize the two musicians were men. But in spite of her anger, she accepted the role, wanting to appear in a film once more.

Before she left for Hollywood to film the movie, according to Lena, she "was in a blind rage for days. All she did was eat. I never saw anyone eat so much in a day, including hamburgers, home fried, four cups of chocolate pudding and a big veal cutlet. She went from 115 pounds to 140."

But the food seemed to calm her, as did the songs she learned for the movie. She would sit on her bed strumming a new ukulele she learned to play, memorizing the lyrics. Lena said Marilyn loved to sing, did it effectively, thanks to Fred Karger who at least taught her how, even though he had refused to marry her.

She prepared to leave for Hollywood, join director Billy Wilder, whom she disliked, feeling he had shown little respect for her during the filming of *The Seven Year Itch*, her twenty-fourth film, made in 1955. Wilder said of her disparagingly in a Life magazine article in 1960: "She has breasts like granite and a brain like swiss cheese, full of holes. The charm of her is her two left feet."

He told Maurice Zolotow, who wrote *Marilyn*, "I'm the only director who ever made two films with Monroe. I think the Screen Directors Guild owes me a purple heart." But after Marilyn died he praised her as "a great actress."

"You are as good as the best thing you have ever done," Jack Lemmon quoted Billy Wilder as saying, as Lemmon spoke of Wilder's genius at both writing and directing films during *The Kennedy Center Honors: A Celebration of the Performing Arts*, held at the Kennedy Center in Washington, D.C. on December 28, 1990. Wilder, along with Katherine Hepburn, was one of those honored that evening in the program on CBS.

Wilder evidently felt both pro and con about Marilyn, varying in his opinion. After her death he said, "I miss her. It was like going to the dentist, making a picture with her. It was hell all the time, but after it was over, it was wonderful."

Asked if he would undertake a third project with her, he said, "I have discussed this with my doctor and my psychiatrist, and they tell me I'm too old and too rich to go through this again." He never made the third film.

He also said, "God gave her everything. The first day a photographer took a picture of her she was a genius," and another time he admitted, "The greatest thing about Monroe is not her chest. It is her ear. She is a master of delivery. She can read comedy better than anyone else in the world."

She occasionally dared express her rage at directors. She worked for twenty-four prominent ones including Huston, Wilder, Olivier, Joshua Logan and Fritz Lang. She was both terrified of the director-father figure and in awe of him. He reminded her of the father who would not acknowledge her but wiped her off the face of the earth.

Before she left New York she learned she was pregnant again, appeared to be delighted, according to Lena. When Marilyn returned from Hollywood after completing the film, she told Lena the experience had been a "nightmare." She "cursed like a truck driver at the dinner table arguing with Miller before it was released." He praised her, having seen some of the filming, "for being funny." She retorted, "I don't want to be funny. Everyone's going to laugh at me. I look like a funny fat pig. A freak."

But when the film appeared, it was a hit as both audience and critics praised it. Thirty years later, it is still shown on television repeatedly.

Marilyn attended the premiere in New York after drinking champagne all day. The audience, knowing she was present, stood and cheered wildly at the end of the film. It made a fortune for Billy Wilder. Marilyn owned a small percentage, which eventually helped her estate become solvent. Lena noted she consumed ever greater quantities of alcohol and pills, in spite of being pregnant.

The studio now suggested Marilyn star in *Let's Make Love*, with Yves Montand, the story of a French billionaire who poses as an actor in a play he financially backs and in which he falls in love with his star.

Before she left to make the film Marilyn suffered her second miscarriage on December 17, 1958, as surgeons at the Polyclinic operated on her. She wrote Lena that all she did while in Hollywood was work and "the nicest thing for me is sleep. Then at least I can dream." She could feel happy only in the fantasy world of dreams. The realities of her life—the failed marriages, the loss of two babies, the failure of Marilyn Monroe Productions—added to her rage at the unhappy direction her life had taken.

She confessed to Lena she did not think she was the woman for Miller. He needed an intellectual, somebody he could talk to as he did easily with Simone Signoret, the wife of Montand. The two couples each took a bungalow next to each other at the Beverly Hills Hotel in

February, 1960, as the filming of the picture started. Miller soon returned to New York, continuing his work on the script of *The Misfits*. Simone left for France to star in a scheduled movie.

Montand and Marilyn then indulged in their affair, taking the title of their film literally. She believed he would leave his wife to marry her. He soon informed her he would never leave Simone but that he had "a nice time" with Marilyn.

She sank into a deep depression at this rejection. It was then she got in touch with Dr. Greenson, told him she needed help, planned to move back to Hollywood after the filming of *The Misfits*. Frank Taylor, Miller's former book editor, and at that time editorial director of Dell Books, had been enthusiastic about Miller's script, suggested Marilyn contact John Huston to direct the project. Huston accepted and United Artists and Seven Arts both financed and distributed the film.

Marilyn's rift with Miller widened before they left for Reno and the on-location filming. Marilyn was ecstatic when she learned Clark Gable would play the part of the cowboy who became her lover. She had adored him since childhood, his picture hung on the wall of her room when she was in the orphanage. Gladys had once shown her a photo of her real father, Gifford and Marilyn thought he looked like Gable.

Lena described a scene in the New York apartment that took place before Marilyn and Miller left for Reno. One afternoon Marilyn walked into her bedroom after talking to Miller in the room where he worked, screamed, then threw a champagne bottle against the wall where it smashed "into a million slivers." Marilyn said in a fury of Miller, "He said it's *his* movie. I don't think he even wants me in it." Then she viciously slammed the closet door open and shut. Lena thought she would break it off.

Miller had told Marilyn his nerves, as well as hers, were frazzled, that he could not deal with her lateness on sets, her drinking. He also could not stand Paula Strasberg's constant presence on the sets. He added he did not want to keep embarrassing himself as he apologized for Marilyn's problems, made excuses for her appearing late. He suggested that unless she could be professional, perhaps she should not accept a part in the film and "foul up" his project. Marilyn reported to Lena she had never believed he would hurt her this deeply, she had now completely lost faith in him.

She begged Lena to accompany her west for the filming but Lena could not leave her two children and husband, who had injured his back. Marilyn then phoned Lena regularly from Reno, as she promised, related her many miseries on the set—it was too hot, the food was inedible.

Her anger mounted, she could no longer successfully conceal her rage at Miller, the two barely spoke to each other. Increased consumption of alcohol and sleeping pills prevented her from reaching the set on time and she kept everyone waiting for hours, then had to go through many retakes. Most of the cast and crew were angry except Gable and Montgomery Clift who sympathized with her, knowing her marriage was exploding.

Huston planned to direct the movie *Freud*, starring Clift, as his next picture. He asked Marilyn before she left the set of *The Misfits* to play the lead woman in it, a patient whose legs were paraplegic and could not walk but through Freud's help was able to face her emotional conflicts and then found she was no longer paralyzed, could easily move her limbs.

On her last day of filming in Reno, November 4, 1960, Marilyn told Huston she decided against appearing in *Freud*, saying,"I can't do it because Anna Freud doesn't want a picture made about her father. My analyst told me this." She was referring, of course, to Dr. Kris in New York, a close friend of Anna's, who knew Freud had been against any interpretation of his life and work to the public, except what he wrote. Anna wished to fulfill his wishes, she told Dr. Kris, who, in turn, told her patient Marilyn. She suggested Marilyn, soon to leave her and move to Hollywood, not appear in the film.

When Marilyn returned to Manhattan she informed Lena that Miller would no longer reside at the apartment, announcing, "It's our house now, Baby Lamb."

The day Miller walked in to pick up his typewriter, books and papers, Marilyn locked herself in her room. She had expected him to be the saint who would save her. At this time it appeared Marilyn started to give up on life to some degree. If the move to New York had not offered magical results, nothing else would. Failure with Miller meant somehow she was headed for a tragic fate.

Christmas is always a time of depression when, as adults, we find ourselves alone. Marilyn now faced a loveless Christmas in 1960. Lena suggested Marilyn call DiMaggio to cheer her up, as he often did on the phone and with occasional visits. She talked nearly an hour and a few days later he arrived to join her for the holidays. They were affectionate, Lena reported, Joe calling Marilyn "darling," taking her out, discussing new films for her as scripts arrived daily. When DiMaggio was compelled to leave for Florida and the annual baseball practice before the season started, she once again felt deeply depressed. DiMaggio never seemed to give up the belief that she might return to him one day.

In February, 1961, Marilyn thought seriously of killing herself. Gable's wife had been repeating the charge that Marilyn had caused Gable's death because of the many retakes in the hot sun of Reno. One afternoon Marilyn suddenly felt the wish to throw herself out of the window to the street thirteen floors below. She walked over to the window, overwhelmed by the impulse to commit suicide. Then she decided not to jump. She told Dr. Kris of her strong wish when she next saw her.

It was then Dr. Kris had committed her to the Payne Whitney Clinic and Marilyn, in a state of panic at being treated as though she were insane, phoned DiMaggio and once again the hero, he raced to her rescue. Dr. Kris then had transferred Marilyn to Columbia Presbyterian Hospital where she was given a private room minus bars at the windows and a locked door. Marilyn told Lena she had at last slept without the help of a single pill or glass of vodka. "Not one bad dream," she announced in triumph. The drinking and the pills brought out the rage and hatred in her "bad" dreams. Unfortunately, there are no known records of what these nightmares focused on. But like all dreams they held the terrors of the past, from childhood on.

At this time Marilyn became close to Frank Sinatra, he gave her a pair of emerald earrings and a little white poodle she named "Maf," short for Mafia. She told Lena she expected Sinatra to marry her. She also confessed that in her early Hollywood days she only required of men with whom she slept that they be "nice." Added, "If it would make them happy, why not? It didn't hurt me. I like to see men smile."

She may have believed promiscuity did not "hurt" her but a promiscuous woman sooner or later harms herself because of guilt at sleeping with so many men. Her reputation suffers eventually, her image of herself declines. Marilyn's sense of self esteem, exceedingly weak to start with because of the lack of parents, eventually became even weaker as the men with whom she slept started to think of her as a plaything, refusing to marry her.

This included Sinatra, Montand, President John F. Kennedy and finally, the President's brother Robert. In the last years of her life she headed for men at the top, unaware of the peril in it for her. She wished to marry, establish a permanent, trusting, lasting relationship but was unable to do so because she could not trust a man nor be trusted herself. This is "the great sickness of Hollywood," says one psychoanalyst who lives there and has treated many stars, both male and female.

Following *The Misfits* (and was Miller saying in his choice of title what he thought of his wife—a misfit, at least in marriage?) Marilyn seemed at last to accept that audiences wanted to see her and to laugh with her, as in *Some Like It Hot*, a money-winner the world over. She asked Lena constantly, walking nude before her mirrors, "I look pretty good for an old lady in her thirties, don't I?"

In a sense she now felt like "an old lady". But she had felt like one too when she was a little girl, facing a hostile world. Any child deprived of parents so early in life grows old swiftly. She also had to be a parent to herself in many ways, primarily in the emotional areas and thus flew into adulthood prematurely without ever experiencing joy in childhood.

She seemed to possess somewhat of a confidence in herself until the summer of 1961. Then problems with digestion led to a gall bladder operation. The long, prominent scar on the right side of her stomach seemed to plummet her into depression. It was the first overt blemish on her body, a mean-looking gash that took months to heal and then left a permanent scar. She also thought her breasts were growing flabby and her face showed an occasional line. This terrified her, according to Lena, as it would any woman who placed her complete faith, her virtual survival, on how her body appealed to men.

"I don't want to get old, Baby Lamb," she cried out to Lena. "When my face goes, my body goes. I'll be nothing...nothing...over again." Tears ran down her face.

Age to her meant the madhouse, no way to escape it. She could not face her rage as a girl of eight when her mother went "mad" and deserted her completely.

Now she was truly alone once more, except for Dr. Greenson. She hoped he could be the rescuer she had sought from day one.

She once wrote the poet Norman Rosten after she returned to Hollywood following the uncertain years in New York:

Help, help,
I feel life coming closer
When all I want to do is die.

This said it all. It signalled her eventual suicide. Her wish could not have been clearer had she taken out an advertisement in the newspapers proclaiming, "Help me! Help me!"

🐞 🐞 🐞

Marilyn now felt that her effort in New York to be a wife to Miller had failed dismally and she was growing too old to continue her success in the films. Her inner rage was starting to bubble, as it had when she had not been able to control it at times with Miller.

She was afraid to face the buried fear and anger in her sessions with Dr. Kris, and now Dr. Greenson. All patients are hesitant to reveal their forbidden, hidden desires when they start analysis. Such wishes are concealed in the first place because we are taught they are taboo. Some patients never fully acknowledge these wishes if they fail to gain a sense of trust in the analyst and subsequently in themselves.

Women often choose to marry angry men who act out the rage and fury the woman dares not express. Marilyn did this in the case of DiMaggio who, it was reported, had at times struck her, though never causing lasting physical damage. But this touch of violence would terrify Marilyn, summon to the surface her stifled memories, the beatings with the razor strap in the foster home when she dared to disobey as a little girl.

Her foster parents, she recalled, had humiliated her the few times they struck her. She said she forgave them, remembered them as basically kind people, the way she forgave DiMaggio, who became her constant friend, would even take care of her burial. But we never in our hearts forgive anyone who inflicts even the slightest sign of violence upon us, though we may pretend to do so. Their cruelty and our wish for revenge haunt us our entire lives.

Marilyn now tried desperately to trust Dr. Greenson. She told Lena she was placing all her hope in him with the telling words, "Lena, I've finally found it. I've found a Jesus for myself. I call him Jesus. He's doing wonderful things for me. He listens to me."

When Lena asked what else he did, Marilyn said, "He gives me courage. He makes me smart, makes me think. I can face anything with him. I'm not scared any more. Now, nothing bothers me. I'm so happy."

This is how most patients feel during the first months of analysis. They enjoy what psychoanalyst Reuben Fine calls "the honeymoon period." The patient is not asked at once to examine the rage that lies beneath the surface of his civilized behavior. That follows after he feels more at home with the analyst. The latter knows the depth of the anger and hopes eventually that the patient will dare to face the dark side of his human nature. This includes the wish to murder when we feel someone has hurt us, physically or emotionally or both.

Marilyn told Lena she had learned through her sessions with Dr. Greenson that her marriage to Miller had been "too big a challenge." In trying to win his exalted respect, Marilyn had become obsessed with making her mark in "serious dramatic roles" that were false, not her forté. She wanted now to concentrate on film comedies and musicals, "to be myself," she said. Adding with a slightly puzzled look, "Whoever that is."

Whoever that is! This tells the world that she had never felt a strong sense of the solid self we must all achieve to some degree if we are to make peace with the natural wishes for retribution and violent feelings that stir within, so we may successfully defend ourselves when attacked verbally or physically by an enemy or someone we believe our friend.

Her deep inner and outer anger had slowly mounted over the increasingly unhappy years, as anger always does if intense enough, leading some to commit murder. For Marilyn, it resulted in murder of the self through pills, vodka, champagne. She had not sought analytic help soon enough so she could express the many hidden feelings of anger that lay dormant. Only if those emotions are aired can one be set free from such a traumatic past. Not words, not dreams, not acts, but only the letting go of buried feelings attached to early traumas at the hands of supposed loving ones, dispells the rage connected to the past.

It seemed to everyone that, as a star in her fifteen years of startling success, Marilyn had it all. A short and sweet victory over the enemies of her earliest days. But the depth of the inner fear and fury that she carried with her would not allow her to enjoy success or love one man.

It was too difficult a psychic task for her to make peace with her misery-laden youth. Hers was a childhood in which she felt deserted by both the man and woman who had created her. The race between Marilyn's attempt to understand her justified rage, with Dr. Greenson's help, and her fear of growing old, losing her sex appeal and going mad, was not even a close one. The psychic cards were against her from her very first days.

She was unable to face her deep emotional wounds, know she was entitled to feel consummate anger at her parents and the world's cruelties. Only then could she make peace with her tortured childhood.

Instead, she kept burying her agony, fear and rage ever more deeply, used an increasing intake of alcohol and barbiturates to get through the day and night. This meant she drew nearer and nearer to the darkling chasm of death.

Norma Jean at 8 with a friend
© Robert F. Slatzer

4.
A Childhood
Most Cruel

What were the tortures in Norma Jean's childhood that drove Marilyn to wish to die at such an early age? Who were the original villains that had hurt Norma Jean so severely that the movie star called Marilyn Monroe did not wish to live beyond thirty-six years and two months?

Devastating damage to our emotional life can occur in the first two or three years when we are the most vulnerable. Such is the staunch opinion of leading psychoanalysts throughout the world. Some even say it is the very first year that is most important in setting the emotional foundation for the future adult.

If we are consistently loved and nurtured during these early years by those who care for us, we possess a lasting strength on which we can always rely. But if we fail to receive a consistent sense of love and worth from a mother and father, we are apt to find the rest of life untrustworthy, unrewarding, perhaps even terrifying at times.

Did Marilyn's early years, which she lived as Norma Jean, bring her a sense of being loved and cherished? What clues can we find that connect to her wish to kill herself just as she turned thirty-six?

Norma Jean was born June 1, 1926, at 9:30 A. M. in Los Angeles General Hospital. No father was at hand nor would any father ever be present in her life. "But Marilyn knew that Gifford was her father," Guiles reports. "It was absolutely conclusive he was. Her mother showed Marilyn his picture. Gladys was not ashamed of the fact. Ashamed maybe that her daughter was illegitimate but not that Gifford was the father." There were reports that when Gifford had impregnated divorcée Gladys Mortensen, he had not yet divorced his wife.

Gladys Pearl Baker Mortensen had a son, Emmett Jack, and a daughter, Berneice, by her first husband, Jack Baker. He left her, it was rumored, because she had an affair with another man. Gladys lived for a while with her two children at her mother's home, then moved to a rented room in Hollywood. Shortly after, Baker's relatives, living in a rural section of Kentucky, offered to be the legal guardians of the two children Gladys was unable to support. When she entered Los Angeles General Hospital to give birth to Norma Jean, she listed her two earlier children as "dead," as no doubt they seemed to her in a far-off Eastern state.

Before Norma Jean was conceived Gladys had married a second time, Edward Mortensen, a native of Norway. He had no steady job, worked as mechanic, then as a builder's helper. Gladys was usually able to pay the rent but he was unreliable, often jumping on his motorcycle and disappearing for days. Suddenly Mortensen deserted Gladys, moved to San Francisco. She broke the lease on the cottage they had shared, moved into a furnished room. As her mother had done, and her new daughter Norma Jean would later do, Gladys selected men who subsequently abandoned her.

Gifford, Norma Jean's father, as her mother later informed her, worked as salesman for the film laboratory at Consolidated Film Industries. Gladys worked there five nights a week as head film cutter. Her job included splicing together processed negatives for some of the leading film companies. Gifford, in his thirties, was six feet tall, possessed broad shoulders and a trim mustache above a wide, sensual mouth.

One day in the fall of 1925 Gladys went to her mother's house and confessed she was pregnant but the man would not marry her. She then asked if she could live with her mother after the birth of the baby.

She could not take care of a baby and continue to work, she needed the job to survive. Gladys also did not want her fellow tenants in the house where she rented a room to know she had an illegitimate baby, as the Bolenders, Norma Jean's first foster parents, told Guiles.

Della Monroe Grainger refused her daughter's request. Della explained she had problems of her own to solve with a husband who had suddenly left for India without his wife. Six months before Norma Jean was born, Della set off for India in December, 1925, to join her wayward husband. She had rented her bungalow to an insurance salesman and his new bride. In late May, 1926, Gladys went into labor, was rushed to the hospital and on June 1, Norma Jean was born.

She proved to be the easiest of Gladys' three births, Norma Jean later told the Bolenders. The new baby seemed healthy, alert and normal. When Gladys' co-workers learned that Gifford would not contribute a cent to his daughter's birth, they raised $140 to help pay the hospital bills. Gladys nursed Norma Jean, the name on her birth certificate, written by Gladys—the full name was Norma Jean Mortensen. Mortensen was not her father but his name was used temporarily as Gladys tried to legitimize her daughter by giving her at least the last name of her second husband.

After eleven days in the hospital, Gladys took her baby to the home of Ida and Dwight Wayne Bolender via taxi to Hawthorne. The Bolenders, for five dollars a week, acted as foster parents to small children. Her baby in her arms, Gladys left the taxi to enter the home of the Bolenders. Guiles described the town of Hawthorne as "a working-class flatland near what is now Los Angeles International Airport."

Gladys knew of the Bolenders' business because they lived across the street from Glady's mother, Della. Gladys believed that if Norma Jean were placed in this foster home, Della would be able to see her grand-daughter regularly, be available if needed. Gladys intended to visit both her baby and her mother dutifully every Saturday, traveling to Hawthorne by trolley.

Norma Jean's grandmother was a disciple of evangelist Aimee Semple McPherson, who had triumphantly opened her million-dollar Angelus Temple in Los Angeles. Della was a recluse and did not make friends easily. Except for trips to the Angelus Temple or the store for basic staples and foods, she was rarely seen outside her house. By the time Norma Jean was born, Della had spent twenty-two of her fifty years in California. Born Della Hogan, she and her family had moved from Missouri to Hollywood where she met her first husband, who claimed to be descended from President Monroe. Their marriage, resulting in the births of Gladys and her brother, Marion, ended in divorce. After marrying late, Glady's brother Marion, was committed to the state mental hospital in Norwalk, where he eventually died.

Della married a second time, a man remembered only as Grainger, who worked for an oil company. Around 1921 they had moved to Hawthorne, to the house where Della now lived. Grainger was transferred to India that September, some of the neighbors believed he planned the transfer to put distance between himself and a difficult wife. But she intended to join him when she could save enough money for a first-class ticket.

Left alone in Hawthorne, a deep depression gripped Della, the start of what would soon be diagnosed as "manic-depressive psycho." Within two years she indulged in outbursts of fury at neighbors and delivery boys, lived all but in total solitude. Grandmother Della, too, had a lovely face, her eyes, a mixture of blue and green, shone with empathy when she felt friendly. Before Norma Jean's birth Gladys would visit her mother regularly on Wednesday evenings, taking the trolley, waiting for her mother to return from her midweek prayer service at the Angelus Temple.

The studio scene in Hollywood into which Norma Jean was born underwent a dramatic change as it was swiftly converted to sound technology. The Warner Brothers were filming *The Jazz Singer* with Al Jolson, even as the play ran on Broadway. The films of Greta Garbo, Constance Bennett, Colleen Moore and Gloria Swanson were popular. Richard Dix, John Barrymore, Adolphe Menjou and John Gilbert were among the leading men.

Hawthorne, Norma Jean's first home, with its fields and wooded areas, could have been a thousand miles from the film industry. The Bolenders had come from rural areas. Ida grew up on a small farm near Buffalo, New York. Dwight Wayne Bolender, who preferred to be called "Wayne," lived as a boy on an 80-acre farm in Brown County, Ohio. After marrying, the couple settled on two acres in Hawthorne. When Wayne was not working as a letter carrier, he would crank out religious tracts on a printing press in a shed attached to his house. Ida busied herself with the foster children, the pet rabbits and baby chicks she kept in the back yard.

When Gladys occasionally slept over, she and her baby occupied a rear bedroom. Gladys seemed to suffer when anyone hurt her but never dared strike back, afraid to show her fury (as Norma Jean would later be afraid to show hers), according to the Bollenders. Some Saturday nights Gladys would return early to Los Angeles, twenty miles to the north, for a date. She was in search of a third husband with whom she could make a home for her new baby.

It was reported that at times Gladys was difficult to talk to, possessed few women friends. But she remained committed to her life's work, no matter how traumatic the personal crises that arose. Her daughter, Norma Jean, would show this same professional dedication as an adult, though in a far more exalted status in the film industry. We might say Norma Jean breathed the air of filmdom from the day she was born, not only because she lived near Hollywood but because her mother was so involved with the stars and the industry.

Occasionally Gladys would be seen weeping for no apparent reason, sometimes she would laugh unaccountably. Marilyn later recalled her mother feeling lonely, isolated and rejected (as Marilyn herself would feel). But Gladys gave her baby what little love she could. When she stayed overnight, she attended church on Sunday with the Bolenders, carrying Norma Jean in her arms. The little girl rarely cried, she possessed a singularly good nature, the Bolenders told Guiles. A good nature she carried into stardom, for the most part.

In late October, nearly a year to the day after Gladys announced her pregnancy to her mother, Della returned to Hawthorne. She had suffered ten disastrous months in India, was sueing Grainger for divorce, charging desertion. She persuaded the tenants to whom she had rented her house to break their lease and she moved back in.

She appeared "enchanted" with her new granddaughter, the Bolenders recalled, often crossed the street to visit Norma Jean. One day Della saw Ida spank Norma Jean for throwing a bowl of food on the floor. Della harshly admonished Ida, "Don't ever let me catch you doing that again!"

Della would often take her granddaughter to her own home once or twice a week in the afternoons. Ida was concerned, she told Guiles, knowing of Della's sudden temper tantrums, but she dared not interfere with a grandmother's wishes.

During Della's abortive stay in India, Aimee Semple McPherson had gone for an afternoon dip in the Pacific Ocean and disappeared. Reports had it she was drowned, kidnapped and finally a story ran that was later verified—she had run away with the lean, handsome operator of the Angelus Temple radio station. Sister Aimee's disgraceful (to her supporters) behavior caused Della to give up all but Sunday morning attendance at the Temple. And she insisted her granddaughter be baptized in the Foursquare Gospel Church. The six-months-old baby was baptized Norma Jeane though the "e" on Jeane would come and go as she learned to write her name. She could claim to be truly a daughter of Hollywood from that moment on.

❦ ❦ ❦

At thirteen months Norma Jean could talk. One day she mimicked Lester, two months younger, another of the foster children at the home and Norma Jean's first childhood companion. Later, Lester would be officially adopted by the Bolenders. This was a blow to Norma Jean but Ida assured her she could not be adopted because she already had a mother, whereas Lester had never known either of his parents.

The day Norma Jean mimicked him she had addressed Ida, who was bathing her, called her "mama." Ida replied, "I'm not Mama. I'm Aunt Ida. *Aunt Ida!* The lady with the red hair is your mama." Since Ida spent far more time with Norma Jean than Gladys did, cooked and served all her meals, even bathed her, it was natural little Norma Jean thought of her as "Mama."

A near-tragedy involving Norma Jean and her grandmother occurred early July, 1927, when Norma Jean was one year and one month
old. She later told Miller of that afternoon, saying, "I remember wak-
ing up from my nap at my grandmother's house fighting for my life.
I fought with all my strength."

Marilyn claimed this was one of the few experiences she recalled
from infancy and remembered that just as suddenly as the murderous
impulse to suffocate her granddaughter had seized Della, it had suddenly vanished. Perhaps Della, for the moment, had been furious at
her daughter for bearing an illegitimate baby, disgracing her own
mother and in her maddened fury thought that doing away with
Norma Jean would eliminate the stigma of "the bastard child."

Della's mental condition rapidly worsened, she even ceased going
to church, seemed to care about nothing. During her Saturday visits
Gladys noticed her mother could not conduct a conversation without
sudden bursts of anger at some imagined slight. Neighbors were well
aware of the hostility Della projected on innocent bystanders. One
newsboy even asked his distribution company to send Della her weekly
bill by mail. He was afraid to knock on the door, knowing he would
receive a vituperative blast without cause.

Early on Saturday, August 4, 1927, Wayne heard a commotion in
his front yard. He saw Della in a fit of rage racing up the walk toward
his porch. He bolted the front door to protect the children. Angry
words spewed out of Della, an incomprehensible stream, though the
subject seemed to be Norma Jean. Ida walked into the living room as
Della viciously pounded the door, told her husband, "Call the police,
Wayne. Hurry!"

Within a few minutes a black patrol car pulled up in front of the
Bolender home. The two policemen, seeing Della trying to break
through a panel of the door, jumped out of their car, subdued her,
dragged her to the black car. The Bolenders recalled she threw her
head back as though praying to God for help.

She was taken to the state mental hospital at Norwalk, dying only
nineteen days later on August 23 of a heart attack. Gladys chose the
grave site, secured a pastor from the Angelus Temple for the services

because her brother Marion was too distraught to help. Marilyn's ancestors were not happy people. Her maternal great-grandfather, Tilford Hogan, hanged himself at eighty-two. Her maternal grandfather, Otis Monroe, died in a mental institution of general paresis, a form of insanity provoked by syphilis in its final stages.

Gladys' childhood had been a horror, one reason she could not be an adequate mother. Her parents fought constantly, her father was a violent man. She recalled a night he hurled a defenseless kitten against the wall, killing it instantly. With insanity running so openly through the family it is no wonder Norma Jean feared it. Though some believe insanity is inherited, psychoanalysts insist it is not a matter of genes but of the child's absorbing the behavior and sensing the violence within his emotionally disturbed parents. Every child believes his parents are gods, know all the answers. The child acts like and copies his seemingly perfect parents. This is not the same as "inheriting madness."

Gladys started to act peculiarly after her mother died, Ida told Guiles. The impact of the death of first her father, then her mother, patients in mental hospitals, and her brother's quickening retreat from reality, began to undermine her own precarious hold on sanity. By this time Gladys was also somehow involved with a brutal man. One afternoon shortly after her mother's funeral, she appeared in Hawthorne to visit Norma Jean wearing dark glasses. When she removed the glasses before a mirror, Ida noticed one of her eyes was bruised and blackened, half-closed. Ida asked Gladys if she felt all right. Gladys nodded, nervously took out a cigarette, the first time she had smoked in the house.

There seems disagreement on how sternly the Bolenders disciplined their foster children. Marilyn once said in the presence of Rupert Allan, her Hollywood press agent for many years, that the Bolenders had good intentions but put emphasis on "salvation and the strap." Allan asked if Marilyn received more whippings than the other children. She admitted she did, added, "I got into more trouble than the other kids."

One day she pushed over the little bicycle Lester was riding, bumping his head on the sidewalk. She earned a whipping with a razor strop by Wayne. When Gladys next visited, Norma Jean buried her face in her mother's skirt and cried, something she rarely did. She told her mother of the whipping. Gladys asked Ida why Norma Jean had been punished, then agreed she had deserved it.

Little Lester repaid Norma Jean by giving her the whooping cough. Gladys stayed three weeks in a guest bedroom, nursing her daughter back to health. With the exception of one other time, lasting three months as Gladys took Norma Jean to her rented home in Hollywood, this was the longest period mother and daughter spent together during the eight and a half years Norma Jean lived at the Bolenders.

Gladys became film cutter at Columbia Pictures on Gower Street, not far from her old job. She also had a new friend to whom she felt very close, Grace McKee, assistant in the studio's film library, who would later become very important in Norma Jean's life.

Norma Jean faced yet another loss when she entered the Washington School kindergarten, a four-block walk from the Bolenders. She and Lester were enrolled and for the first few days Ida accompanied them to the door, then asked an older child who lived down the block to be their guide.

Soon they had still another companion alongside them. A hungry black and white dog had followed Wayne home from the trolley line one evening. Norma Jean was particularly drawn to the destitute dog (also alone in the world), spent long hours playing with him. She named him Tippy and it was accepted that he belonged to her. Tippy followed her to kindergarten, ran around the schoolyard waiting for recess when she reappeared. Life seemed more cheerful for her, she met new play- mates, had a dog of her own and her mother was talking about finding a house they could share, though it might take two years to save enough money for the down payment.

During the spring of 1932 late one night the household was awakened by the blast of a gun somewhere outside but no one got up to investigate. The milkman tapped on the door early in the morning and informed them he had found Tippy's body in the yard.

A neighbor confessed he had remained awake the night before, shotgun in hand, waiting for Tippy, who spent hours in the dark running around nearby yards. The neighbor had complained to the Bolenders that Tippy, in his nocturnal wanderings, would not stop rolling in his garden, destroying the flowers and vegetables. The Bolenders had taken no steps to restrain Tippy. Norma Jean felt stricken by the murder of her first pet. She would later love the puppy Frank Sinatra gave her, whom she named "Maff," for the Mafia, as she loved Tippy.

❦ ❦ ❦

At long last Gladys made good her promise to live with Norma Jean, put her first down payment on a white bungalow in North Hollywood. It stood near the Hollywood Bowl, just off Highland Avenue. Gladys furnished the bungalow with pieces bought at auction, among them a white piano that would become Norma Jean's pride. She had spent the last year at the Bolenders learning to play the piano, with Miss Marion Miller as teacher. Thus early in life she would have the feeling her mother wanted her to love music, make it part of her future. The white piano had formerly graced the Hollywood home of Fredric March and his wife, adding to its movieland value.

In November, 1933, Gladys took Norma Jean, now eight and a half, from the Bolenders to live with her. This was a milestone in her daughter's life. These three months with her mother were ones she would never forget. She lived in new glory as she had her mother all to herself, taking total care of her. She could hold up her head with other children who had known such intimacy with their parents. This was dramatic change in Norma Jean's existence. Her first real emotional security since leaving the hospital where she was born.

To raise needed money for the mortgage payments, Gladys invited an English couple in their sixties to occupy most of the house, keeping but two rooms for herself and Norma Jean. The husband worked as a stand-in for leading man George Arliss, the wife was a registered "dress" extra, used as a walk-on in drawing room comedies starring Ina Claire, Joan Crawford and other stars. Their daughter, in her twenties, lived with them and soon moved up from Central Casting to stand-in for the thirty's star Madeleine Carroll.

It was here Norma Jean's fascination for the movies truly blossomed. She was surrounded at home by four people closely involved with films and film stars, who encouraged her to see every movie. On Saturdays the English actor would walk Norma Jean to Grauman's Chinese Theatre, give her a dime, leave her. Until the box office opened to let her in the theater, she would watch the monkeys on Grauman's wide patio. The Englishman would buy a copy of *Hollywood Variety*, sit on the front porch of their bungalow and read every industry item, a glass of bourbon in his hand (another accepted habit).

Sometimes little Norma Jean would tuck her feet into the footprints of Gloria Swanson, Clara Bow, Rudolph Valentino. Twenty years later she would be invited to place her own footprints in the courtyard cement as she promoted the opening of *Gentlemen Prefer Blondes*.

She would often sit through a film several times and if it was a musical memorize the songs. She must have felt in heaven, finally living with her mother and enjoying the fantasies of filmdom, a world in which her mother now shared an important role—magical release from serfdom into never-never land for Norma Jean. An end to the acute loneliness she had felt from the day she was born.

It was no accident Marilyn Monroe rose to the top of the film world. It meant her survival, her path to the feel of permanence, a sense of identity she once felt during those three months she lived with her mother and entered the world that fantasy films provide.

Gladys was working the night shift at Columbia Pictures and on the weekends she had a succession of beaux who attempted to cheer her, failed, and faded from view. Norma Jean, in early life, would thus think it natural to be attracted to one man after another, for a girl follows the sexual pattern established by her mother and/or father.

In spite of her victory at finding Norma Jean a real home, Gladys started to feel increasingly depressed. Perhaps she was still mourning too deeply the death of her mother or she was uneasy with her daughter in a day-to-day situation. Gladys had not been able to cope with raising her other two children, she seemed to possess great dif-

ficulty accepting the role of mother. The situation no doubt also revived memories of her own unhappy childhood with a very strange
mother and father.

It was undoubtedly all Gladys could do to live alone, her moods
known only to herself. And now, though she searched diligently, she
could not find a husband willing to help her finance the house and
take care of her illegitimate child.

One morning in January, 1934, while Norma Jean was in her class-
room at the Selma Avenue School, Gladys called in ill to the studio.
Her depression had reached a point where she had now become hysterical, lost control of her rational thoughts, was screaming at the English couple .

At a loss, the Englishman phoned Grace McKee, told her the situation, asked what he should do. Grace advised him to call an ambu-
lance at once.

When the attendants walked into the house, Gladys fought them
off violently. She was strapped to a stretcher even as she screamed
in protest, taken to the hospital where she had given birth to Norma
Jean eight years before. She was diagnosed as "paranoid
schizophrenic," sent to the Norwalk state mental institution in which
her mother had died seven years earlier.

The emotional illness that destroyed her mother and brother had
finally caught up with Gladys, as she had feared. When Norma Jean
returned from school that afternoon, the Englishman took her hand,
said gently, "Your mother was taken ill today. She's gone to the hospital for a while."

This was a time of deep distress and insecurity for Norma Jean.
Once again she had no home, no mother. Now she was forced to face
the stigma of her mother being carried away to a mental hospital.

The English couple, who had become fond of Norma Jean, told
Grace they would stay on, take care of her as Grace donated small
sums for Norma Jean's expenses. On Grace's advice, to help pay the
mortgage on the house, they sold most of Gladys' furniture, including the precious white piano she had bought for Norma Jean.

A year later, when Norma Jean was nine, she became a "county child," as the county subsidized her, naming Grace McKee as her guardian. The English couple had decided to return to their homeland. At this point Mr. and Mrs. Harvey Giffens, whose daughter had become a friend of Norma Jean's at school, offered to take her into their large ranch house in the North Hollywood hills. Giffens worked for the Radio Corporation of America as a sound engineer. Norma Jean was happy to be with this family and after several months Giffens wrote Gladys, asked if he and his wife could adopt Norma Jean and take her with them to Mississippi, where he had been offered a more lucrative job. But Gladys saw this as a threat to the only relationship of any value left in her life. She called Giffens herself from the mental hospital, informed him Norma Jean was not up for adoption.

Grace then decided to place Norma Jean in the Los Angeles Orphans Home, which stood on El Centro Avenue in the heart of Hollywood. Norma Jean, now almost ten, was taken to the home by Grace, who virtually dragged her into the main hall as Norma Jean screamed, "I'm not an orphan! I have a mother!"

She feared to live in what, to her, proved a terrifying place, lost among a horde of girls and boys. She was now a nobody, her home with the Bolenders had been a safe haven as compared to this hell of lost children.

But at least through a window near her bed she could look across the playground to the huge sound stages and water tower of the RKO studios and dream of her mother. This lessened the pain of being suddenly propelled from the freedom of living with her mother, then the English couple, then the Giffens, to the harsh regimentation of an orphanage.

She was awakened at 6 A.M., had to make her bed and help straighten out the dormitory. After breakfast, it was off to a public school four blocks away. Luckily there were no uniforms, she could wear plaid skirts, wool or cotton sweaters.

Her only link with her former life was "Aunt" Grace, who sent the lone birthday card Norma Jean received on June 1, 1936, her tenth birthday. Grace also appeared on Saturdays to take Norma Jean shopping in downtown Los Angeles for small necessities or paid a beauty parlor to give her straight light brown hair a marcel. Often the two would go to a movie over the weekend.

Grace was now being courted by a man ten years younger, Erwin "Doc" Goddard. He was a six-foot-two research engineer for the Adel Precision Products, manufacturers of airplane parts. Recently divorced, he had custody of his three children, two girls and a boy. Grace had promised Gladys on one of her visits to the mental hospital that she would take Norma Jean out of the orphanage where she was so unhappy but she was not yet ready to do so. She hoped to marry "Doc" and move into his house in West Van Nuys, where there would also be room for Norma Jean.

After she had been at the orphanage twenty-one months, Norma Jean asked the matron where her mother was now. The matron replied, "She's away. She won't be coming back." Norma Jean then asked, "Do you mean she's dead?" The matron did not answer. A frightening time for Norma Jean.

She now begged Grace to take her out of the orphanage, said she far preferred a foster home. Realizing how desperate Norma Jean felt, Grace convinced the Directress of the Home that Norma Jean needed substitute parents at this crucial time of her life. Norma Jean finally left the place where she daily helped wash one hundred plates, one hundred cups, one hundred knives, forks and spoons three times a day, seven days a week and also cleaned bathtubs and toilets, went to school, did her homework and was in bed by nine, lights-out time.

Grace found her a foster home in Compton where the husband had his own business making furniture polish and his wife, with Norma Jean by her side, would drive in a battered Chevrolet over back roads looking for hardware stores that would buy the white bottles. In less than a month, Norma Jean told Grace, she knew the name of every village in Los Angeles County. She said she would never forget the sound of the wife's crying out to her every morning, "Norma Jean! Let's go! Lock the door as you come out."

Norma Jean was placed in several more foster homes during the next few years. One turned out disastrously if we are to believe the story Marilyn told several times as an adult, once to Lena Pepitone. She started off, "I had at least one parent. But she didn't want me. I was too ashamed to try to explain it to the other kids at the orphanage."

She went on, "I never felt like I belonged, even at the Home. The only time I was happy was when they took us to a movie. I loved movies. That was the only fun I had. The stars were my friends. That was my freedom."

Thus at the age of ten and from then on, she "loved" movies, they meant "freedom," her only joy in a life sadly void of happiness as she bounced from foster home to foster home after she convinced Grace anything would be better than the orphanage.

Marilyn then described to Lena a terrifying night when she was fifteen in one foster home. The mother had taken the three other children who lived in the house to a movie. She left Norma Jean to study for the next day's English class. The foster child found herself alone with her foster father.

He invited her into his bedroom to talk, handed her a small glass of whiskey. She confessed to Lena, "He had never really talked to me before. It felt good to have someone pay attention to me."

He started to kiss her on the lips and, she admitted, "At first it was nice to be held close and kissed. No one ever kissed me that way. But then...then he wouldn't stop. I thought I had to do what he said. Whatever he said."

She had been trained to take orders from foster parents ever since she could understand one word. He ordered her to take off her clothing and she did. Then he removed his trousers, led her to the bed, stretched her out on it, lay on top of her.

She told Lena, "I didn't scream. I didn't do anything. It hurt a lot at first, then I didn't feel anything. I lay there and just cried."

This foster father was the first man to want her in a sexual way and she was frightened. After she missed several menstrual periods, knowing she would have to tell someone, she sought out Grace.

In Marilyn's words to Lena: "I was afraid she'd kill me when I told her. But she didn't get mad at all. She just took me to a doctor. Later on, I went to the Los Angeles General Hospital where I had the baby...my baby. I was so scared but it was wonderful. It was a little boy. I hugged him and kissed him and kissed him. I just kept touching him."

She shook her head sadly, went on, "I had him in the hospital for a few times. But when it was time for me to leave, the doctor and a nurse came in with Grace. They all looked real strange and said they'd be taking the baby. It was like I was being kicked in the head... I begged them, 'Don't take my baby.' But Grace gave me a dirty look and said it was the best thing. She said I was too young to take care of it, that I had caused enough trouble and to shut up. So they took my baby from me...and I never saw him again."

In this way Marilyn repeated what her mother and father had done to her—abandoned her. In her mother's case, Norma Jean would not, as a child, understand the reason for her mother's sudden complete disappearance into a mental hospital. To her, her mother deserted her because she was a "bad" child, a belief common to all deserted children.

Just after this loss Grace, now Mrs. Goddard, took Norma Jean into her new, large home. Norma Jean attended Emerson Junior High School, a year behind most children her age because of the irregularity of her school attendance. But she appeared to thrive. Norma Jean once again felt safe, she lived with friends once more because Grace had been so close to her mother, Gladys. But Marilyn's early seduction could have impelled her to wish ardently for sex, man after man.

❧ ❧ ❧

The Goddard family called Norma Jean "The Mouse" because she always sat very quietly listening to what the others were saying, seldom spoke on her own. But in her room, after she closed the door, she later said she would act out the parts she had seen in recent movies such as *Jezebel* or *Marie Antoinette*. As she had done at the orphanage, she kept a smiling studio photograph of Clark Gable tacked to her bedroom wall. Her mother once told her he looked somewhat like Norma Jean's father.

That "The Mouse" would eventually turn into the sex goddess of the film world is not so far-fetched if Marilyn's childhood as Norma

Jean is understood in terms of what films and music meant to her. They represented the scenes of her mother's daily life, a world she could vicariously share after her mother had been taken from her, in a sense, forever.

Acting in a movie during her later years was like getting her mother back. Becoming part of filmdom was returning to the home she once knew before she lost her mother. True, she would find pain in the new world, glamorous though it appeared, just as she found pain in the earlier world her mother had provided for her. She fought as valiantly as she knew how to overcome both the old and new wounds.

For fourteen years she would apparently succeed, with an acclaim few other actors or actresses ever received, an acclaim that is still strong today. But behind the glamorous mirror reflection of acclamation, of fame, she would always see the broken shards of her shattered earlier years.

The ghostly remnants of her painful youth would eventually destroy her as the reality of the agony of her childhood slowly obliterated the fantasies of Marilyn Monroe's dreams of glory. Not even her worldwide fame as the international Sex Goddess on and off the screen could undo the persistent panic of a childhood without consistent love and nurturing, without the daily care of a real mother.

From birth on, perhaps sensing even in the womb she was unwanted, Marilyn learned the feeling of desperation, of anger from strangers (foster parents always remain strangers to some degree), of physical punishment at misbehaving (Norma Jean should never have been struck, as at the Bolenders, but punished in ways that held no violence, such as being sent to her room or deprived of sweets or other pleasures).

Most of all she felt the deprivation of a father and to a lesser extent, of a mother. She suffered from what psychoanalysts call "soul murder," the murder of our inner, tender soul.

Her short life was like a murder mystery, as every suicide is. Who does the suicide really wish to kill? In most cases it is the mother and father of childhood, sensed to be angry, hateful, powerful villains. In Norma Jean's case it was the uncaring, absent, unknown father and

the mother who was little more than a child herself, and an angry one—
an anger that would later show in her daughter's heart, now turned,
as the mother did, upon herself. Marilyn's parents had to share in
her wish to self-destruct.

ご ご ご

At the age of eight and a half Norma Jean underwent what was
perhaps the cruelest blow of all when her mother was taken in a strait-
jacket to a mental hospital. From then on, for the rest of her life she
would rarely see her mother. They were to all effect, permanently
parted, though Grace occasionally took Norma Jean to the hospital.

There ensued a definite sense of strain between Norma Jean and
her mother. She later said, "I never really knew my mother. When I
visited her in the hospital she would act as if she didn't know me." It
is never easy for a child who has been hurt early in life by a parent's
absence to understand the conflicts within the parent that have prevented him or her from becoming a loving, nurturing father or mother.

From the day Gladys took Norma Jean to the Bolenders, Norma
Jean knew no consistent love such as that which a mother who is constantly on the scene gives her child. This vital ingredient for happiness
was completely missing. Marilyn's later wish to seek oblivion through
alcohol and drugs stemmed from an early life that gave little assurance anyone wanted or loved her.

A child copies the adults with whom he grows up. Any kind of alcohol was taboo in the Bolender home. Later on, however, Norma Jean,
at the age of eight, absorbed the habits of the English couple who drank
freely, smoked regularly, talked films non-stop and constantly played
records. The daughter gave parties at the bungalow, where life to
Norma Jean had to seem exciting and inviting. Unconsciously, in some
ways she may have copied the couple who took care of her for a year
after her mother disappeared.

Norma Jean lost all contact with the Bolenders after they attended
her wedding to Jim Dougherty when she was sixteen, chosen for her
by Grace. "Doc" Goddard had found a better job in the East and Grace,

who would remain Norma Jean's guardian until her twenty-first birthday, arranged for her to marry the handsome boy next door. After Marilyn became famous she telephoned Wayne Bolender, called him "daddy" as she occasionally did as a child. He ended the strained conversation, according to Guiles, by telling her, "You come see us, Norma Jean," but she never did nor did she phone them again. Perhaps her memories were chiefly unhappy ones.

At times Gladys took extended visits into the world outside hospital walls, once even briefly remarried. But she never made any attempt to assume the responsibilities of a parent with Norma Jean. The black shadows of despair that would eventually envelop and destroy Marilyn could be seen clearly in her mother and grandmother, two extremely depressed women.

The state of California until 1952 carried the burden of caring for Gladys in mental hospitals. When Marilyn started to earn money, she took over the financial care of her mother, moving her to a private nursing home Rockhaven, in Verdugo. After Marilyn's death, Gladys' needs were met by the $100,000 trust fund left her as part of Marilyn's estate.

Gladys' only son, Emmett Jack Baker, died of tuberculosis in the early 1920s. Her daughter, Berneice Miracle, who lives in Gainesville, Florida, once visited her famous half-sister but they found it difficult to talk. Gladys died of heart failure on March 11, 1984 in Gainesville, outliving her famous daughter by more than twenty years.

Marilyn had to feel deep pride when she appeared in her first starring role, *Niagara*, in February 1953 at the age of twenty-seven. She played a seductive villainess in love with a young man whom she has persuaded to murder her husband, an older man just released from a mental hospital, played by Joseph Cotten—Marilyn must have thought of her mother and grandmother.

Guiles notes that in this film Marilyn's voice had dropped "to a lower register," where it would remain. Her "breathy sexuality, as well as her provocative buttock-swinging gait, her moist-lipped open mouth and her ash blond hair" became from then on a part of her personality onscreen. The film elevated her to the élite of stars who made top money for producers. From then on she fought with the studio for more money. Guiles believes she needed the tension of opposition. It felt familiar as she moved against "contrary forces" all the rest of her life.

Another reason Marilyn chose films as her savior would be the fact her hardworking mother had hardly ever taken her eyes from a movie film, the way she had supported herself. Marilyn found another more pleasurable and challenging way—she became part of the very film itself. Perhaps she fantasized her mother would be watching her, recognized her daughter the star, wish now to love her, stay with her always.

Marilyn inherited her mother's beauty, though not her flaming red hair. She did inherit her mother's slim figure. Though Gladys was not often present in a physical sense during Norma Jean's childhood, she always remained present in the girl's fantasy of herself, both body and mind.

She seldom spoke of her mother in later years, she seemed ashamed of her because of her frail mental health. Though Marilyn rarely saw her mother, she would still feel a deep bond, as does every child his mother.

After her success in *Niagara* the unwanted child now had it all, a short and sweet victory over her enemies, over life itself, at least temporarily. But the emotionally cruel childhood she had endured, causing ongoing turmoil within, would not allow her to enjoy success, love one man, make peace with the miseries of those first years.

Norma Jean never knew who she was—even her film name was not her own. Renamed Marilyn Monroe, she became more split emotionally. According to psychoanalysts, the change of name a movie star often undergoes makes him feel he is at least two personalities— his old and his new. This sometimes ends in disaster, as attested by the number of suicides committed by actors and actresses who had name changes.

It seems clear Norma Jean early in life received the message her mother wanted her to become a movie star. Gladys' profession was dedicated to film cutting, part of her love for the stars. She told her little daughter she had named "Norma" after Norma Talmadge, then in the limelight, of her passion for screen celebrities. Marilyn may have unconsciously or consciously followed in Norma Talmadge's footsteps all the way, including the heavy drinking and the consumption of barbiturates.

Marilyn's conscious goal seemed to emanate from the desire to show the world she could be a success, win every man's love as she attained the wish of her mother and her own strong childhood wish. Her pictures also strengthened her strong fantasy to remain in childhood. Films in those days portrayed chiefly the childish, not the adult part of life. They centered on dreams and fantasies, not realities, as many of the current films now do.

Marilyn had no choice in choosing her films, the studio led the way. But at first she was content to play in any movie chosen for her as it awakened her strong fantasy to have her mother by her side, reminiscent of the times Gladys took her little daughter to Saturday afternoon movies, then returned her to the Bolenders. "Movies" and "mother" were merged in Marilyn's mind.

In *The Magic Years* by Selma H. Fraiberg, the title refers to childhood. She states that without a mother to constantly care for them, children spend their infancy and formative years in what she describes as "an impoverishment of the personality, as if a nutritional deficiency had affected the early structures and devitalized parts of the personality."

Fraiberg points out that children "who have never experienced love, who have never belonged to anyone, and were never attached to anyone except on the most primitive basis of food and survival, are unable in their later years to bind themselves to other people, to love deeply, to feel deeply, to experience tenderness, grief or shame to the measure that gives dimension to the human personality."

When Marilyn was a little girl and begged Ida Bolender to allow her to call Ida "mother," Ida would not allow this. Marilyn could not understand such an arm's-length stance. She was fed, clothed and taken care of daily by Ida, seeing Gladys only once a week on Saturdays. To Marilyn, Ida felt more like a mother than her own mother.

Because of Ida's response, Marilyn would feel like an outsider in the house where she spent the first eight years of life.

There was no mother's touch in Marilyn's daily life, no one to whom she could appeal for comfort when hurt or puzzled or upset in any way. In the important formative years of her life, when all our experiences are deeply imprinted in memory and influence the rest of our lives, Norma Jean felt a complete outsider, lacked consistent love from anyone. She was always the stranger in the house where she lived.

Fraiberg also points out that what she calls "the unattached children" are slow to acquire a sense of personal identity, of "I-ness in the full sense of the term." When the "I" emerges as word and concept it is a late acquisition by the standards of family-reared children and retains the "blurred and uncertain quality of a two year old's 'I' far along the road of development, in some cases permanently."

The need to develop a strong sense of "I" is important, she says, because it is the "integrating factor in personality development. The sense of personal identity is the concept that binds the feelings of self and the differentiation of one's own body, thoughts, subjective reactions from persons and objects outside the self."

Infants are not born with this sense. In the early weeks they do not differentiate between their bodies and other bodies, between their mental pictures and real objects outside them. The average child does not acquire the word and the concept "I" until the middle of the third year. When this concept emerges, it brings with it a great improvement in the reality sense of the child—"a sharpened differentiation of self and not-self, of inner and outer, subjective and objective, and a corresponding shift from the magic or wishful thinking that characterizes infancy to the rational thinking that characterizes mental processes."

Before there can be differentiation of self and outer world, the latter must have a representative, Freiberg declares. She explains, "A child who lives in a world of insubstantial and shifting human objects and is unbound to any of them will have difficulty in forming a stable image of himself. And because human objects, the first 'realities,' are unsatisfying and impermanent, his reality sense is correspondingly poor."

The child will have difficulty, as Marilyn did, "in differentiating between inner and outer subjective states and reactions and objective conditions. This does not mean he is mentally ill—a far more complex state—but it does mean his personality is marked by tendencies to distort, to employ magic or wishful thinking far beyond the age at which we normally find primitive thought in children."

It also means, Freiberg adds, that the child is slow to acquire knowledge about the world around him or develop a coherent, organized view of "the tiny piece of earth he inhabits." These unattached children like Marilyn, "are unstable children, highly vulnerable to all kinds of mental pathology and in later life contribute to the ranks of the mentally disordered to a frighteningly large degree."

The ability to control impulses, triumph over our sexual and aggressive urges is one of the most "distinguished achievements of man," Freiberg concludes. It is dependent every step of the way on ties to the ones who have brought us up, educated us emotionally. If such ties between the child and his educator are lacking, unstable or shifting all the time, the child has great difficulty in achieving the most elementary forms of control of feelings and wishes.

Looking at Marilyn's childhood we can understand her later feelings of acute loneliness, ones she had never been without. She felt deprived, neglected, as indeed she was, needed to drink unceasingly to escape the terror, pain and rage of both her childhood and adult life, then swallow pills to be able to sleep.

To make up for this excessive, lifelong need she sought and received love from the masses as she exuded on screen a sexual appeal based on innocence and guile. In effect she begged, "Please love me, I am so very much in need of love."

Not all film critics obliged. Pauline Kael wrote of Marilyn, "Her face looked as if, when nobody was paying attention to her it would go utterly slack—as if she died between wolf calls." As part of her mind probably did when she left fantasy for cruel reality.

Another time Kael became even more critical: "She would bat her

Bambi eyelashes, lick her messy suggestive open mouth, wiggle her pert and tempting bottom and use her hushed voice to caress us with dizzying innuendoes. Her extravagantly ripe body bulging and spilling out of her clothes, she threw herself at us with the off-color innocence of a baby whore."

Marilyn's deepest secret was her fear of growing old, then losing her mind, when no man would want her. This was what she saw her mother do when Gladys was turned down by several men as she searched for a father to her baby, found none, went insane.

❧ ❧ ❧

Except for brief periods Gladys remained confined until after Marilyn's death. Inez Melson, eventually appointed Gladys' guardian, said, "She was overly taken up with her religion, Christian Science and with evil. She figured she had done something wrong in her life and was being punished for it."

Marilyn estimated she lived in ten foster homes before she was sixteen. In some she stayed only a few months. A happy child she was not, since the hour she was born, almost every moment filled with anxiety, the feeling of being unloved and facing a world of strangers day after day.

As Freud pointed out with reference to both his patients and himself, anxiety seems to accompany the act of narration, especially when the narrative is an attempt at reconstructing childhood history. The latter is often obliterated in memory but remains forever a deep, desperate fear.

A description of the child's denial in fantasy and acts was given by Anna Freud in 1937 in *The Ego and the Mechanisms of Defense*. Such denials are normal in childhood but evidence of severe disturbances if they persist. She said, "I suppose we tend to call it defensive when the child prefers to turn to such denial in fantasy or in action to an unusual degree, at the expense of coping with the real world."

Quoting Dr. Joseph Sandler, a well-known British psychoanalyst, she added, "On the other hand, people who use denial a great deal in adult life are very threatened by reality, because if they meet reality directly, and the reality does not fall in with their method of coping, they suffer very badly."

All her life Marilyn unconsciously "disavowed" the truth of her exceptionally painful past. Freud described disavowal as a process which in the mental life of children seems neither uncommon nor very dangerous but which in an adult would mean the beginning of a psychosis. Marilyn could not accept her inner agony, it was too terrifying to face consciously.

Marilyn never achieved womanhood. She lived like an adolescent. She did not possess the mature mind needed for a lasting marriage. Her body was her whole reason for being. She hated underwear, wanted to be a nude child, loved for her body. She later said that she often had the desire, when her mother occasionally took her to church, to take off all her clothes, stand in the nude. As though it were the only way she could arouse love and caring.

Dr. Zve Lothane, well-known psychoanalyst, author of the forthcoming *In Defense of Schreber*, to be published by The Analytic Press, says of Marilyn, "She had an inability to accept herself as she grew older. She wanted to be the eternal usual beauty, preserved and untarnished. With this concept of the self, you want to die young to preserve it.

"Marilyn was not just a sex symbol or a dizzy blonde. The audience identified with her as embodying the ideal of narcissistic perfection for men and women alike. They also became aware of the latent tragic aspects of her life—she was fragile and vulnerable, that was her appeal. A combination of these physical and spiritual qualities will continue to strike a universal chord in the reading public."

But whatever the extreme to which Marilyn went, she was never able to make up for her acute early losses, or to mourn them. This meant they would continue to devastate her ever more deeply.

Successful mourning entails facing the loss, feeling the grief, allowing the tears to pour out, as well as coming to terms with the rage we feel toward those who have abandoned us. If we cannot accept this, the mourning becomes even more intense and we never make peace with the loss.

Marilyn's numerous abortions would affect her life deeply. Father Robert McGuire, Jesuit Priest, a counsellor who does therapy, lives in Nassau County, New York, describes what he calls the Post-Abortion Syndrome and how he has helped women suffering from the act of abortion.

"We deal with the mother as she becomes conscious of what she has done," he explains. "We help her pray in a supportive way, ask God and the child for forgiveness. We point out that God is merciful and forgiving as we personalize the child not fictionally but in reality. I speak for the child, point out the child would never have been conceived if the mother had not wished for and accepted it. Mothers cry and weep as I thank them. The result is a transformation in the personality of the mother, as if she were cleansed. She had never given herself a chance to repent, believing she had committed the unforgivable."

He adds, "We deal with the mother as she becomes conscious of her feelings. The gift of repenting for not giving human life. The essence of the child never dies as in a sense the mother takes possession of the child, feels it will be alive in eternity, which thus appeases her tremendous loss."

Marilyn castigated Norma Jean for getting pregnant—her father had done this to her mother, chastised her by abandoning both her and the baby. The aim of Norma Jean's dreams was to replace the child she had lost in her teens. Judging by at least fourteen abortions, we can assume Marilyn was repulsed at the thought of bearing a child, believing it would end what, to her, was her most precious possession— her career. She also unconsciously feared she would be unable to bring up a child as her mother and father had proved themselves unable to do with her.

Marilyn's repeated abortions were a vital force in fighting Norma Jean, the innocent within, who finally fought back at the price of Marilyn's life. How many abortions could one woman stand? This was a gruesome way to punish the self.

Marilyn could not make peace with her traumatic losses, however. Her inability to go through the important mourning process connected to the early loss of her father, then her mother, was clearly evident in the last years of her life.

She was telling the world in the words of her hero Clark Gable, tossed contemptuously to Vivien Leigh in *Gone With the Wind*, "Frankly, my dear, I don't give a damn!"

If a child has not experienced the love and understanding of his needs by a parent, he will not, as an adult, possess the feelings of love and understanding to give others. In no way could Marilyn offer a mature love to any man who entered her life. But at least, perhaps because she had started analysis, she survived four and a half years with Arthur Miller, her longest marital relationship with a man.

Norma Jean at the orphan home
© Robert F. Slatzer

5.
Descent
Into Terror

Marilyn once screamed at Jane Fonda as they talked, "I'm never going to get old! Getting old means going crazy."

This was her deepest fear. That she would go mad and wind up like her mother, taken away at the age of thirty-four to a mental hospital where she would spend most of the rest of her life. Marilyn was telling Jane Fonda and the world she had promised herself not to live long enough to "go crazy."

How old was Marilyn when, under the alias "Miss Faye Miller," she was placed behind bars at the Payne-Whitney Psychiatric Clinic in New York? Also thirty-four.

This was not just mere coincidence, it reveals how embedded in our unconscious lies our most terrifying fears, ones that often come true if we do not face and conquer them. Like mother, like daughter is a powerful progression. Marilyn was the perfect example of how rigidly we copy our earliest models, our parents.

A year and a half after the Payne-Whitney trauma, in which Marilyn clawed at the bars of the hospital window, screaming in agony, she would take her final overdose of barbiturates. She preferred death by her own hand to living death in a mental institution.

During her life she professed to love a number of men but never felt at peace with one because she could not feel at peace within herself. Her mind was in constant turmoil, flooded by memories of the past. She had little chance to "choose wisely," instead she was driven by compulsive fantasies and wishes.

While most of her directors maligned her for holding up production, impatient with her constant delays and her dependence on acting coaches, one director wrote only of his deep admiration for her. Joshua Logan, director of *Bus Stop*, praised her highly, did not mind her late arrivals on the set of her twenty-fifth film. Many believe, as Logan did, *Bus Stop* to be her finest movie. In his 1978 book, *Movie Stars, Real People and Me*, in the chapter "Will Acting Spoil Marilyn Monroe?" he offers the most sympathetic portrait any director ever gave her.

Logan admits he had been warned Marilyn might be difficult, notes that he nearly missed one of the high spots in his life as director because he almost listened to the popular Hollywood prejudices about Marilyn. He was also warned not to let acting coach Paula Strasberg on the set, informing Marilyn this would not be permitted though she could consult Paula in her dressing room.

Logan spoke of Marilyn as possessing wit, wisdom, patience and the ability to co-operate, describing a side of her most other directors did not see. During the filming of *Bus Stop* he gave a picture of her that showed Marilyn at her performing best: "I found Marilyn to be one of the greatest talents of all time. She was always the most beautiful person in the room, and certainly the most fun to talk to, to listen to—warm, witty, and with the enthusiasm of a child. Innocent, yes, but she was never ignorant, stupid or gross. She was in my opinion extremely bright, totally involved in her work. I think she was at some kind of peak in her emotional as well as intellectual life."

He thought the work she had done with Paula and Lee Strasberg greatly stimulated her. She talked constantly of Constantin Stanislavsky, wanted to know all the details of Logan's studying with him in Moscow. Logan wrote, "I think that Lee had opened a locked part of her head, given her confidence in herself, of her brainpower, in her ability to think out and create a character. But sometimes she acted as though she had discovered something that no one else knew."

He explained that because of her experience in analysis words like "Freudian slip" and "the unconscious" and "effective memory" would appear in her conversation "at the oddest time." He added, "But she was never so serious about herself that she didn't give her remarks a kind of wistful, comedic twist."

It seemed to him, he wrote, that Marilyn was a combination of Greta Garbo and Charlie Chaplin—he caught both the comic sense in Marilyn and the beauty and sexual appeal she possessed. He said she was so lovely she could have played almost any romantic part suited to her and yet he also believed "she could have put on those baggy pants and that little mustache and made a fortune with slapstick and a sad, tearful twist."

He pointed out there were certain "great actresses, even great beauties" who seemed rejected by the film medium, their power of acting lessened by it, but Marilyn played "with feverish concentration." The moment the camera was turned on, "it was just as though someone had pressed a button; she was immediately acting." No distraction could keep her from playing the part until she heard the word "cut." He says of her, "She was owned by the camera."

He mentioned the comments of directors and actors on her inability to remember lines. He admitted in some scenes with lengthy exchanges of dialogue there was some difficulty "but never because of memory, only because of anger and frustration."

Bus Stop was filmed chiefly in the vast complex of buildings on the Twentieth Century-Fox lot in Los Angeles. The final day of shooting the cast traveled to the snowy Idaho hills to do the "bus stop" scene, in which Don Murray, playing a cowboy who seeks desperately to marry Marilyn, the slightly promiscuous singer, wakes her up in the morning after they have shared the night together.

He said, as the camera focused on them, "Wake up, Cherie, no wonder you're so pale and scaly," meaning she seldom saw the sun, slept past noon.

Logan ordered the cameraman to stop, said, "Wait a minute, cut!"

He turned to Don, explained, "Don, I'm terribly sorry but you said 'scaly' instead of 'white.'"

"Oh, Lord, I'm very sorry," Don apologized.

They had to reload the camera. Logan sat down on one side of the bed in which Marilyn had supposedly been sleeping naked. The sheet covered her body. He heard her voice, "whispering and exciting," coming from the head of the bed.

She said, "Don, do you realize what you did? You just made a *Freudian* slip."

Then she raised herself from the bed, still covering her body with the sheet, "with a look in her eyes that showed she was in the midst of an intellectual experience," Logan wrote.

She explained further to Don, "You see, you must be in the proper emotional mood for this scene because it's a sexual scene, Don, and you made a Freudian slip about a phallic symbol. You see, you were unconsciously thinking of a snake. That's why you said 'scaly.' And a snake is a phallic symbol. Do you know what a phallic symbol is, Don?"

He replied, "Know what it is? I've got one! "

Logan summed up, "It was the perfect nonmeeting of the minds." Malapropic or not, it showed Marilyn had acquired the language of psychoanalysis, at least the intellectual kind of approach some patients use as a way of blocking their terrifying, hidden thoughts from emerging.

But the use of psychoanalytic "jargon" never helped a patient feel better. Only by experiencing her emotional reactions to the traumas of her early life could Marilyn unburden herself of long-buried fear, rage and grief. If she were unable to do more than intellectually talk about her analysis after four years with Dr. Kris, we may assume she did not feel any relief from her lifelong anguish. It appeared she had been too emotionally destroyed in childhood to be helped in such a short time, as Dr. Greenson's first meeting with her would later indicate when he asked her to sit in a chair and face him rather than start off by lying on the couch.

When Logan next saw Marilyn in London with her new husband for the filming of *The Prince and the Showgirl*, she was "a different person," he said. For the first time she openly showed "her fangs." He went to her dressing room to greet her but she would not let him past the door. She looked as though she were furious.

She tried at first to be gracious, said, "Thanks for what you said about me in *The New York Times*," where words were favorable. Then added angrily, "But why the hell did you cut out that scene in the bus? I'll never forgive you as long as I live. I was going to show it to Arthur and I couldn't. I was never so angry in my entire life, and I'm just as angry now as I was then!"

She closed the dressing room door in his face. He wrote that he understood exactly how she felt, that he had also been upset. He wanted to keep the scene, on which both of them had worked hard but it had been ruled out by a superior at the studio. He felt he could never be able to adequately explain to her why it was cut, for he himself did not know, and she obviously did not want to talk further about it.

Logan also mentioned that co-star Laurence Olivier gave her a "bad time." At one point Olivier took him aside, said, "Thank you so much for writing all those letters. It was terribly thoughtful of you— but, my God, why didn't you tell me it was going to be like this?"

Logan asked, "How is it?"

"That beast Paula Strasberg is on the set all the time, and every time I do a take, Marilyn looks at her to see whether or not we should print it." Olivier was the director as well as playing the leading male role.

Logan said to him, "But, Larry, I told you not to let Paula on the set."

Logan also told Olivier that he thought Marilyn was "terribly talented" and "on intimate terms with the camera." He reminded Olivier, "You have every facet of acting, directing, drama, the whole theatre art is yours. All she has is brilliant instincts and the mystery of a frightened unicorn."

"Unicorn" is a bit too mythic to describe earthy Marilyn but she did possess the mystery of a frightened, uncertain girl whose earlier life was emotionally horrendous. The portrayal of Marilyn possessing a "horn," interestingly enough, also indicates Logan thought of her as masculine and dominating at times, for the horn, indeed, is a phallic symbol.

Logan wrote that Olivier was accustomed to a prescribed way of working with well-trained, obedient co-workers and "you can't teach an old director new tricks." Logan also knew that the many sugges-tions by directors "rolled off Marilyn's back like so much water." He recalled John Huston did not like the way she sneered at Miller dur-ing *The Misfits*—by that time she had made up her mind to leave him. But, Logan wrote, he never saw a "mean side" to her and "All I know is that together with her I hit my peak, and as far as I'm concerned, she hit hers."

When he and his wife Nedda read the news of Marilyn's sudden death they felt shocked "because both Nedda and I had grown very fond of her and we both felt that *Bus Stop* linked her to us with a strong emotional tie."

He recalled the last night of shooting when Marilyn invited Nedda and him to Trader Vic's restaurant in Hollywood for a farewell din-ner. She was waiting for them with a package, handed it to them. It contained a large photograph of her in a silver frame. She had in-scribed in white ink, "With love and thanks to Nedda and Josh from Marilyn." Milton H. Greene had photographed her in an old cos-tume from the Twentieth Century-Fox collection, she looked like a beauty from the turn of the century. She also presented them with a dozen yellow roses.

When Marilyn died and Logan called Paula and Lee to talk of the loss of someone they both loved and respected, Paula said, "She loved it, you know." He asked, "What?" She explained, "The silver frame of the photograph she gave you." Marilyn thought so much of Logan and his wife that she had given him one of her own most prized pos-sessions.

In his book he also says Marilyn struck him as a much brighter per-son than he had ever imagined, this was the first time he learned "that intelligence and, yes, brilliance have nothing to do with education." He praised her reading of "good books," her "quicksilver" laugh.

He spoke of the night he first met her and she expressed yearnings to be a great actress. She mentioned she wished to play Grushenko, the sensual girl in *The Brothers Karamazov*. Then added, "She's very erotic, you know."

Logan commented in his book that the only thing on which Marilyn felt herself an authority was "eroticism, anything that suggested sensuality or sexuality gave her instant, joyful confidence." Delicate as were her skin and coloring, Marilyn at heart was "a physical girl. Whenever the subject of sex came up, there was a twinkle in her eyes. Sex was obviously fun and infinitely desirable. Up until her new educational phase, sex had been her finest hour."

Why was Marilyn so aware of her sexual feelings? There were several reasons, as there usually are to explain why we act in a compulsive way about anything excessive in our life.

For one, Marilyn probably carried out her mother's seductiveness. Gladys was known to have left her first husband for another man and to date many men while searching for a father for her baby. How mothers react sexually is reflected in the daughter. Who else is there to copy in the first years of life? If you watch a baby carefully you see how he imitates the expressions on his parents' faces, their movements as he learns to crawl and walk, their voices and words as he develops speech.

For a second reason, when Marilyn was a child she dwelt in a world of fictional romance and love as her longed-for mother took her to the movies on Saturday afternoons. When she lived three months with her mother she saw films constantly. This continued after she was forced into the orphanage at nine, when Grace would pick up her up on Saturday, head for the movie theatre. Seeing a film for Marilyn as a girl was no doubt her greatest joy, propelled her toward a fantasy-land featuring sexual themes.

In a sense Marilyn was like the children of film stars who follow the same career as their parents. Gladys cut films so America could see on screen the sexual love affairs between men and women. Her daughter later visualized herself playing such roles.

For a third reason, Marilyn seemed to carry out her mother's unconscious, if not conscious, wish that her daughter become an actress. As mentioned earlier, Gladys gave her daughter the name "Norma" because of her admiration for Norma Talmadge. It is interesting that Talmadge's first husband, Joseph Schenck, many years later would propose to Marilyn, trying to tempt her with the eighty million dollars that would be hers on his death. Marilyn may have felt during the short time she knew Schenck on an intimate basis that she replayed the oedipal triangle, taking "papa" from "mama."

Another early strong fantasy may have been Marilyn's belief that if she became the sexiest woman in the world no man would leave her as her father had so mercilessly done. To her he was as good as dead and her mother had become lost forever when she entered the world of fantasy in which the mentally ill dwell. Marilyn probably made up her mind very early in life this would *never* happen to her. As she announced to Jane Fonda, she would never, never become like her pathetic, helpless mother.

❦ ❦ ❦

Realizing some of the emotional traumas in her life, Marilyn had finally sought a psychoanalyst. But psychoanalysis is not a "get rich quickly" process emotionally speaking. A patient as disturbed as Marilyn may take many years to understand the reasons for the buried, blind furies whirling within.

Because of the lack of a family during her entire adult life, Marilyn acted out one of her most intense unconscious fantasies. She created the Sex Goddess, the woman no man would abandon, all men would desire. "All men" stood for the first man in her life, Gifford, who had repudiated her when she lay in her mother's womb.

She called her husbands "daddy," do we need more obvious proof than this? But she also had a far stronger *unconscious* wish to get even with her father—to be the one to leave the man.

When a man left her, she felt denigrated, depressed, deserted. But when she left a man she felt victorious, justified, avenged.

Dr. Greenson became alarmed at Marilyn's increasing trend toward what he wrote his colleague was "random promiscuity." Marilyn's mother had gone "mad" when it appeared she could not find a man who would marry her, become the parent her eight-year-old daughter needed. She obviously engaged in many affairs in her search for such a man. Hollywood is known for the quick and easy "revolving door" of love.

Marilyn once told Dr. Greenson that one night she had invited into her home a workman who was engaged in remodeling her house and had sex with him. Still another night she did the same with the taxi driver who brought her home from a party. An undercover investigator for the Los Angeles District Attorney, engaged in another case, told of stumbling on Marilyn in the act of sex with a man in a darkened hallway during a Hollywood party.

Dr. Greenson maintained the vital separation of doctor and patient in their relationship during her sessions. Marilyn, however, became a close family friend. He believed this the best he could do, he did not want to send her to a mental hospital, as Dr. Kris had, knowing the terror this would create. He also knew she could not cope with being alone because of her fear of going crazy.

He wanted her, if possible, to slowly try to face the unpleasant truths that would set her free from her overwhelming addictions and allow her to sleep drug-free. Truths about her rage at her mother and father. Her utter loneliness as she grew up feeling no one really cared about her. Her consuming sexual need—any human port during still another emotional storm.

Our two strongest drives, both deeply affected by the amount of love and the kind of nurturing we receive in childhood, are the sexual (love) and the aggressive (hate). We learn to control both our sexual desires and violent feelings if we grow up with kind, caring parents. But without parental care both the sexual and violent feelings may explode later in life, out of the control of reason.

In her later years Marilyn not only used obscene language at times but allowed some of her rage to surface, temporarily becoming "the gutter girl," as she once referred to herself. This is one way a woman may feel more like a man, who easily tosses off what we call the foul words.

Dr. Greenson noted she took great offense at the slightest irritation on his part with her self-destructive behavior. She could not stand the notion, he said, that "certain ideal figures in her life," including him, found fault with her. He wrote his colleague, "Marilyn could not rest until peace had been reestablished."

Her inability to handle anything she perceived as a mild hurt or critical remark (which, he hoped might be an "interpretation" designed to help her become aware of a destructive act and halt her depression) "were ultimately the decisive factors that led to her death."

Dr. Greenson wrote in December of 1961 that she was going through a severe depressive and paranoid reaction. "She talked about retiring from the movie industry, killing herself," he said. "I had to place nurses in her apartment day and night and keep strict control over the medication, since I felt she was potentially suicidal. Marilyn fought with these nurses so that after a few weeks it was impossible to keep any of them."

Her address book for this period listed thirty-six doctors to each of whom she went in emergencies for her sleeping pills. He later wrote that within days of her death, "I should have played it safe and put her in a sanitarium, but that would only have been safe for me and deadly for her."

A month before she died, in July, 1962 she was secretly hospitalized in Cedars of Lebanon Hospital for four days, reportedly undergoing an abortion. This may have been the result of her affair with Robert Kennedy, though she had sex with other men, as Dr. Greenson pointed out. Why did she refuse to take precautions? Why did she so often inflict upon herself the pain of an abortion as punishment for her guilt, both for the affair and for what many women feel is the murder of their baby?

Perhaps she did not wish to bear a child who would have to endure the fear and rage she did. She also might not have wished to raise a child alone, as her mother did and then go mad. Or was she, in a sense, wreaking vengeance on the "father" of the unborn child?

This last abortion appeared to be one of the final psychological burdens in her life, perhaps the straw that broke her remaining courage, her will to go it alone any longer.

She wrote David Conover at this time that she felt she was through with films, too old to go on. This meant, in her fantasy, she could only "go crazy." But she preferred to die alone in her home, not after years in a mental hospital as her mother, grandmother and.grandfather (the one who killed the cat by hurling it at the wall) had done.

❦ ❦ ❦

Gladys had lived once again for a brief time with Norma Jean when, after twelve years in the Norwalk Hospital and before the emergence of Marilyn Monroe, Gladys was considered well enough to rejoin normal society. Norma Jean was preparing to make a name for herself in modeling. She used her savings to rent a two-room apartment in West Los Angeles and asked her mother to share it.

This was the second attempt by mother and daughter to become closer and proved just as ill-fated as the first, which had lasted three months. There were times Norma Jean would leave the house for weeks on an extended modeling assignment, had to leave Gladys alone. After seven months of trying to live together, Marilyn moved into the Studio Club in Hollywood and Gladys asked to be recommitted to Norwalk. This same inability to be alone as her mother had shown was evident in the last months of Marilyn's own life.

Aware of her daughter's growing rise in the film world, Gladys wrote to her from the Norwalk Hospital in 1952, "Dear Marilyn, Please dear child I'd like to receive a letter from you. Things are very annoying around here and I'd like to move away as soon as possible. I'd like to have my child's love instead of hatred. Love, Mother."

After Marilyn's death Gladys became even more disturbed, attempted suicide by stabbing herself with hairpins, then tried stuffing bed sheets down her throat. In 1963 she reportedly escaped from Rockhill by lowering herself from a closet window, walked fifteen miles to the Lakeview Terrace Baptist Church in the San Fernando Valley. She was discovered twenty-four hours later holding a Bible in one hand, a Christian Science handbook in the other and was taken back to the sanitarium.

Three years later Gladys contacted her daughter, Berneice, in Gainesville, Florida. Berneice sent for her, became her mother's legal guardian in 1967. Gladys was well enough to move to a retirement home in 1970, near her daughter, her first independent residence since 1935.

Inez Melson, Gladys' former guardian, once said, "We seldom talk of Marilyn, with her mother's belief in the hereafter, she does not regard her as dead but, rather, in heaven." Gladys once remarked, "I'm not interested in material things only in God."

❧ ❧ ❧

As 1962 started, at Dr. Greenson's suggestion Marilyn at long last bought the Brentwood house, establishing her first independent home. Perhaps she remembered that her mother, before she lapsed into madness after buying the bungalow, had lasted only three months. Marilyn would last six months and four days.

She now also purchased a car at Dr. Greenson's suggestion, so she could drive the mile to his house for sessions and also to the beach house in nearby Santa Monica owned by Peter Lawford and his wife Patricia (née Kennedy), who had become her friends.

Marilyn had met Lawford through Sinatra, both men part of the "Rat Pack" (the name tells us something of what the members thought of themselves). Lawford appeared to use the beach house when his wife was not present, as a love nest for the Kennedy brothers. Jeanne Martin, wife of Dean Martin, another Rat Pack member, later wrote of Lawford that he played the "role of pimp for Jack Kennedy."

Like every child, who starts life feeling eternal and omnipotent, Marilyn would also think it her fault that she had driven her mother insane and that one day she would pay by going mad herself. As night follows the day, every child whose parent loses his sense of reason feels he is to blame, that somehow he could have prevented the tragedy. This leads to unbearable guilt.

There was a fatal connection between Marilyn's early crippling childhood and the growing intensity of the fear, fury and anguish that caused her attempted suicides, ending in a final one that succeeded as her undercurrent of rage and fear finally conquered her will to live.

All her life she buried the wish to kill those who had hurt her, hurled the murderous wishes swiftly into the dark part of her mind. The price she paid for not facing hidden wishes was the essence of suicide. As long as we become aware of the hidden wishes we believe forbidden, we will not need to act on them. They lose their power as they become conscious.

From the public's viewpoint Marilyn had everything to live for—fame, beauty, money, all the men she craved. This enabled her to make it through thirty-six years. But by then the curtain of darkness that had kept her from feeling a sense of emotional courage had become too impenetrable for her to go on.

Dr. Harold Greenwald, Clinical Professor of Psychiatry at the University of California at San Diego, points out "fame is never enough" for anyone who seeks it believing it will bring happiness. He adds this explains why an actor will still feel deeply depressed, even commit suicide, after he has achieved international fame and possesses all the money he needs.

"What he really seeks is the love of someone he feels will care for him deeply, like a mother cares for a child," Dr. Greenwald explains. "The childhood of many Hollywood actors and actresses, like Marilyn experienced, has been lacking in this kind of care if you study their early years. They seek the impossible in later life."

He adds,"There is an interesting contradiction in Marilyn's life and the lives of other actors and actresses. Although she achieved fame and fortune this made her feel even more depressed as she buried her anger. It was 'bitter ashes' so to speak. When you have achieved fame, you know it's not enough, that you still live in the vacuum of unrequited love.

"Marilyn kept telling herself, 'Someday I *will* find someone who will take care of me, emotionally and physically.' This had been missing from the time she was eleven days old and her mother took her from the hospital to a foster home. The subsequent story of her life shows she never found anyone who really loved and cared for her. Her demands were too great for any man or woman to fulfill."

André de Dienes, one of the finest still photographers with whom

Marilyn worked, in his 1986 book *Marilyn Mon Amour* with its stunning photographs of Marilyn, wrote of their visit to her mother in 1945: "Norma Jeane's mother lived in an old hotel in the centre of Portland in a depressing bedroom on the top floor. The reunion between mother and daughter lacked warmth. They had nothing to say to each other. Mrs. Baker was a woman of uncertain age, emaciated and apathetic, making no effort to put us at our ease. Norma Jeane put on a cheerful front. She had unpacked the presents we bought: a scarf, scent, chocolate. They stayed where they were on the table. A silence ensued. Then Mrs. Baker buried her face in her hands and seemed to forget all about us. I was distressed. She had obviously been released from hospital too soon."

At this time he was "madly in love" with Marilyn, talked of marrying her when she got her divorce in Las Vegas from Dougherty. He took her back to "Aunt Ana's" home, where she was temporarily staying. Ana Lower, a woman who never married, had adored Marilyn ever since she gave away the bride at Marilyn's marriage to Dougherty on June 19, 1942, and had consoled her after the marriage broke up. This was possibly the most loving relationship Marilyn would have in her life—the maternal care she had never received from her mother.

Shortly after Norma Jean's release from the orphanage she lived with Aunt Ana for the first time for a short while. Aunt Ana introduced her to the Christian Science Church. Marilyn once wrote Maurice Zolotow of Ana, "She changed my whole life. She was the first person in the world I ever really loved and she loved me...I once wrote a poem about her, it was called 'I Love Her.' She never hurt me, not once. She couldn't. She was all kindness and all love."

In the late 1940s Norma Jean wrote Clarice Evans, her one-time roommate at the Studio Club, "There's only one person in the world that I've ever really loved. That was Aunt Ana...Aunt Ana was sure—surer than I am now—that I was right in my ambition to be an actress and that I'd be a success. But she'll never know whether she was right or wrong. She died before my first bit part." Aunt Ana died before Marilyn had achieved any real celebrity as an actress, something Marilyn would have enjoyed her seeing.

De Dienes finally realized Norma Jean would never marry him when she told him "softly" over the phone one day, "But André I don't want to get married. I want to get into movies."

He said he felt like committing suicide but did not, became "just a good friend to her...We would never be strangers." He photographed her over the years, said he taught her "how to make the most of herself, how to project herself, to put herself across in public... Thanks to me she discovered her best profile, toned down her laugh and learned to stand up, sit down and hold out her hand, all done with the utmost propriety and provocativeness."

He persuaded her, he said, to be seen everywhere, "never to say no to photographers," convinced her all that mattered was that the public should see as much of her as possible. For a girl who had grown up unloved, unappreciated, this must have been an emotional balm, healing and soothing to her oft-squelched spirit.

Just after Norma Jean changed her name, de Dienes described how he was with her when she picked up a pencil and tried out her new name with "two large, curly, romantic Ms on a notepad. She was getting acquainted with her new identity, saying 'Marilyn Monroe' as if tasting a piece of candy."

He added, "From then onwards no one was allowed to call her by any other name. Not even me."

Over the years he saw her at times, took her to visit the old Spanish missions dating from the arrival of Christianity in California. Another time he showed her Valentino's monument, she noted he had died in 1926, the year she was born. She protested when de Dienes said "those whom the Gods love die young." Marilyn insisted she wanted a long life even if she *never* became famous. But then added that she had a feeling her life would be short.

De Dienes commented knowingly, "She was twenty and had never experienced the intoxication of success, yet already there was a shadow over her radiance, in her laughter."

It was not all sweetness and light between them. At times he would become angry when she demanded he come running if she needed him, then forget that he existed for weeks on end if she were busy. He told her this, she replied she had never asked him for anything, quite the opposite, she felt she had been too submissive. He noted these were "the last sparks from a love affair, brief and violent as a thunderstorm which was to leave its mark on me for ever."

During her marriage to Miller she visited de Dienes one evening looking tormented, huddled in an armchair, bewilderment in her eyes, seemingly "panic-stricken." He told her that he still loved her, had never stopped loving her "both in her splendour and in her days of decline."

Once Marilyn phoned him at two o'clock in the morning, as she was often wont to call friends when she could not sleep. She sounded alone, unhappy, despairing. She suggested he pick her up, take a series of photos with one of the darkened streets of Beverly Hills as backdrop and the car headlight as the only light source.

He asked in surprise, "Now?"

She said, "Yes, right now."

He said he would have refused but he caught a note of desperation in her voice "which made my heart turn over." He jumped out of bed, dressed, grabbed his cameras and dashed off to join her.

She was not wearing any makeup, her hair was dishevelled, her eyes darkened with circles. He tried to find the correct lighting to soften her drawn features, to pick greenery to lessen the squalor of the dust-lined street to which she had taken him, but there was nary tree or bush on it. He wondered if this "sinister dead-end street" was how she saw her future. He did not say a word, wanted to give her a chance to express the anguish and despair that seemed to overwhelm her. It was as if she had a foreboding about some tragic event soon to occur in her life.

After he took the photographs she said in a barely audible voice, "You usually write captions for your photos. You can put 'The end of everything' underneath these."

He described a day in the fall of 1961 when Marilyn had turned up at his home without warning. She was dressed in black and for the first time he noticed she no longer "had that special glow of youth which only a short time before had made her so dazzling." Insomnia, tension, the shock of Clark Gable's sudden death, her separation from Miller, all had left their mark, he thought. She was smiling, seemed calm, but he could tell she felt on edge. She said, "If you're still so keen on taking photographs of me, go ahead. I'm free tomorrow, this evening, this minute. Suit yourself."

He pointed to papers piled high on his desk, the chairs, the bookshelves, even the carpet. She said she was sorry to have bothered him, left without even accepting a cup of tea. He felt ashamed, jumped into his car, headed for the Chateau Marmont where she was staying. He found her in a two-room suite, trunks of clothing everywhere. He wondered if she had just arrived or was preparing to leave. She said she had decided to return to New York, *The Misfits* finished.

He realized, he wrote, "she felt very alone, bereft; I was filled with anguish for her. To have striven so hard for all those years only to end up with such emptiness! Had this loneliness driven her to come and see me on such a trivial pretext?" She took a bottle of champagne from the refrigerator, they each drank in silence. For the first time they seemed to have nothing to say, both worn out, ill at ease.

He wrote that he did not know what to do "about this woman who haunted thousands of men's dreams." In an emergency, she now turned to him, he was the one to whom she had cried out for help. He suggested they go off together somewhere, perhaps to his European homeland, Transylvania. She smiled but did not answer, looked exhausted. When he left, she seemed comforted. As he phoned the hotel the next morning, he was told she had just departed for a flight to New York.

De Dienes last saw her on June 1, 1961, he had first seen her in 1945 when she was nineteen. He now remembered that June 1st was her birthday, read in the papers she was staying at the Beverly Hills Hotel and dialed the number. They put him through to her at once.

Without giving his name he started to hum, "Happy Birthday..." She interrupted, sounded overjoyed, asked, "André, is this you? Come on over at once, let's celebrate."

He found her alone, she had taken out a jar of caviar and two bottles of champagne. Fox had organized a cocktail party in her honor at the studios but she had stayed only a short while, pleaded tiredness. She told him, "They're all against me. When I just can't take any more they think I'm being temperamental. They can't understand what it's like to be so tired that it's impossible to get out of bed in the morning."

He wrote that he knew only too well how badly she was sleeping as her nervous system gave way: "What really upset me about her wrecked life was her bitterness: her success was a sham, her hopes thwarted; she had been let down repeatedly, even by the men who had said they loved her. Her money had been squandered, fame had become a burden."

She told him, "They've all exploited me and now I've got nothing."

He said, "For heaven's sake, Marilyn, it's not the end of the world." He thought, She is a star, people will help her go further, attracted by her fame, others will profit by her successes, and he told her this.

He took her in his arms, searched for her lips. She cried out, protesting, "Oh please, don't! I'm so tired of all that. Don't ask anything of me. You of all people."

There were tears in her eyes, he felt he had been a brute. He knew she had recently left the hospital after a major operation, her gall bladder had been removed. He felt ashamed, said goodbye.

In the street he wondered if she had got rid of him because she was expecting someone else. He retraced his steps, saw her bedroom light go out almost at once, was overcome with remorse at his suspicions.

The next day he sent her a basket of her favorite fruit, before she left Hollywood she dropped off outside his door a selection of her latest photographs. They showed her smiling and radiant, utterly misleading, he thought. He wrote that he "little guessed this was our last goodbye."

Norma Jean at 15
© Robert F. Slatzer

6.
Suicide on the Installment Plan

The facts about Marilyn's life for the most part are well-known. But, ah, the fantasies. It is the fantasies that can kill us if they become too intense, too terrifying. As they killed Marilyn.

No one but her psychoanalysts, Dr. Kris and Dr. Greenson, knew the power of her fantasies though she revealed many over the years to lovers, husbands, friends. Clues lie in some of the many books written about her that describe her fears and feelings. The compound personality Norma Jean/Marilyn seemed to have been scared every day of her existence, no matter how swiftly her popularity mounted.

As the fantasies of Marilyn's life exploded during her last year, she seemed to exist solely on Dom Perignon, vodka, sherry and sometimes as many as twenty barbiturates a day. Felice Earley, who met Marilyn when both were just starting careers, describes Marilyn's life as lived like "suicide on the installment plan."

Felice gave a revealing portrait of early Marilyn, interviewed in the spring of 1989 in Felice's three-story Manhattan house on East Sixty-Sixth Street. She had traveled to Hollywood in 1948 as Felice Ingersoll, a beautiful young woman chosen to appear, along with Marilyn, in the movie *Scudda Hoo! Scudda Hay!*, directed by F. Hugh Herbert. This was the first film for both Marilyn and Felice. Neither were listed in the credits as their parts were too small.

Felice described Marilyn and herself as two of seventeen "starlings" who in 1948 received the annual "Success Award" given by the Honorary Colonels of Hollywood, Post 43, of the American Legion to those "most likely to succeed to stardom." Photographs of the seventeen appeared in the local newspapers. Of the seventeen, only Marilyn, Arlene Dahl and Wanda Hendrix became well known. Felice left Hollywood soon after to marry a man who did not want her to become a film star.

She said of Marilyn when she first met her, "I couldn't make up my mind if she was very bright or very dumb. She once told me, 'We're like comedians. If the audience doesn't laugh at you, you're not very good.'" Felice added, "I decided then Marilyn was bright. You need to be bright to be a good comedian."

Felice described Marilyn as "missing a father...she acted as though pleading, 'I need a daddy.'" Added, "When Marilyn appeared on the screen in *The Asphalt Jungle*, though it was just a small part, everybody in America asked, 'Who's that?' It made her a star."

Felice depicted the camera as "weird and merciless to most people but it loved Marilyn. In the one screen test I saw, she appeared very seductive. She tap-danced around a man and the way she moved came off sheer seductiveness. I wondered, Where did she ever learn this? I never saw a person move as she did. The minute she entered a room she knew how to sell her special aura."

Felice also remarked that Marilyn "achieved what very few of us ever do. She reached her whole potential. Where could she have gone after *The Misfits*? She couldn't have reached greater heights."

But even at this earliest stage of her career, Marilyn's wish to die was strong, Felice said. She explained, "I felt at times she was suicidal, as though death lay underneath her warmth. For she also had warmth. She must have received some love and affection somewhere, from someone." According to Marilyn, who was then Norma Jean, only from Aunt Ana.

Felice reminisced, "The most colorful time of all in Hollywood, I believe, was when Marilyn and I lived there. It's the struggle that is exciting. Success is never easy to handle, as Marilyn found out later."

Felice recalled the day she heard Johnny Hyde, who worshipped Marilyn, hoped to marry her after arranging for her first important films. Felice commented, "People who are vulnerable, like Marilyn, have a quality that makes a man want to do things for her." She added ironically, "I have a different quality. People ask me what I can do for them."

She then said, "Hollywood knew Marilyn had talent. You believed her when you saw her in a film. It wasn't just acting. It came from inside her."

Felice described Hollywood as "both wonderful and difficult. You could take such a moral beating out there. Marilyn must have been given many such beatings. Like a soldier in the war. When you're young and pretty, as she was, your defenses are down."

Felice later learned how desolate Marilyn's childhood had been, remarked thoughtfully, "I remember things from childhood that burned in my mind. You really don't learn much more after childhood; except how to handle your memories better. Every childhood is traumatic, some more than others." Added, "Parents rule by guilt. The most merciless guilt."

☙ ☙ ☙

When Marilyn moved into her own house in 1962 she described it as "a fortress where I can feel safe from the world." Her use of the word "fortress" tells us she felt at war with the universe.

Protected by this self-made fortress, Marilyn remained half-waif, half-woman, her soft, seductive voice that of a young girl entering the world of eroticism with both a smile and a hidden wish for vengeance. She once described herself as "the slum child from Los Angeles" and never really shook that image. As Conover wrote of her, "Marilyn played the best game, with the worst possible hand. Only the rarest kind of courage kept her going to the last."

Another fantasy common to every girl—an exceptionally strong fantasy, since it leads the way to eventual love of the man she will marry—was the wish to possess her father. This natural passion for the parent of the opposite sex could never be emotionally worked through by Marilyn since she lacked a father.

Her first sexual experience, according to her confession to Lena Pepitone, was the rape by a foster parent. Hardly the way for a girl just embarking on adolescence to experience her budding sexual stirrings. It is no wonder her adult life was one of promiscuity, based on that first sexual contact with a drunken, violent man before she was even prepared to handle a normal, loving sexual experience.

She would wish to kill herself after Clark Gable's death because of her wish to kill her father. Though on the set she acted as if she adored Gable, who treated her gently and had understood her plight, when he died this represented abandonment by still another man she both needed and hated, reminiscent of her father. Thus her wish at the moment to kill herself because of strong murderous thoughts.

Men, however, did help in Marilyn's rise to fame. The first was Private David Conover, whose photographic gifts propelled Norma Jean toward her blazing career. Conover had been sent during World War II, on a routine Army photo assignment to take propaganda pictures of women in war work. He was ordered to carry out this mission by no less than Captain Ronald Reagan of the United States Army's Motion Picture Unit, its first such unit. Conover went to the Radio Plane Company in 1945 where he spotted eighteen-year old Norma Jean Dougherty and his photographs of her landed on *Yank* magazine's cover.

Conover was also responsible for sending her on her first modeling agency job. He suggested Emmeline Snively, head of the Blue Book Modeling Agency, which signed Norma Jean to a contract in the summer of 1945. Emmeline recognized the young woman's potential, introduced her to Helen Ainsworth of the National Concert Artists Corporation, the agency that opened the doors to Marilyn's movie career.

Conover later wrote, "I never thought of her as a sex goddess or movie queen. She was a woman, sometimes frightened, often confused; a woman who in many ways was still a child, who with courage was learning to reach out and grow, to mature as an individual and in her art."

He said he felt she kept too much "bottled up inside" and when they met he would ask questions about her childhood. He recalled she said of her father, "I often dream of finding him and going to him or call him. Just to hear his voice, even just to hear him say, 'hello' or 'goodbye' or shout 'get out of my life.' Just to know that he's real and not just paper."

The insecurities of childhood left a deeper mark on Marilyn than showed outwardly, he said, one of the few to ever sense this. More than once he was awakened when she would cry out in her sleep, "troubled by her personal demons." He would gently cradle her in his arms, stroke her hair and murmur, "It's all right, Sweetheart. Don't be afraid. Everything's all right." In the morning she would seem half ashamed, look a little pale, apologize in her shy, soft-spoken way.

He remembered clearly one night when they had just fallen asleep. He was wakened "by a scream so shrill and penetrating that I jerked upright in bed. Norma Jean was sitting beside me, shivering and bathed in perspiration."

She stammered, "It's that nightmare. Those men in white gowns..." then stopped.

"Go on," he said softly. "What happened?" He wanted her to talk about it, believing this might ease her pain.

"They force me into a straitjacket and carry me out of the house. I'm screaming, 'I'm not crazy! I'm not crazy!' but they ignore me." There were tears in her eyes.

Once again she felt the fear of going mad like her mother, a fear not many of those close to her understood or could make allowances for. Also when she was frightened, she would retreat into a "somnambulistic mood," as Conover described it.

He cited Nunnally Johnson, the producer-writer of *How to Marry a Millionaire*, as often the target of her moods at this time. He quoted Johnson as once remarking, "You can't talk to her. Talking to her is like talking to somebody ten feet under water. Between you and her there is a thick wall of cotton. You can't get through to her."

Just before she married Miller, when Conover visited her in Manhattan, she asked him to have sex with her. He said, knowing of her coming marriage, he thought it best to keep their relationship platonic. She burst out laughing, asked, "How in the world would our going to bed together complicate our relationship?"

When his wife Jeanne finally met Marilyn, she told her husband, "My God, she's such a fragile and helpless thing, you want to cuddle and protect her like a kitten." Added, "She's got a lot more than sex appeal. She has sweetness, warmth and lovableness. No wonder you were captivated by her."

That June Marilyn wrote him from New York that Lee Strasberg, who was giving her acting lessons, was recommending psychoanalysis so she could discover and use on stage the deep feelings hidden within her inner self. He became much more to Marilyn than her acting coach—he was her hero, friend, savior, counselor, father figure, and was now convincing her to call Dr. Marianne Kris and start analysis at once.

Conover noted in his diary, "I'm afraid analysis will do Marilyn more harm than good. It will be like opening Pandora's Box, releasing all the ugliness and misery of her childhood that her conscious wishes to forget. The result could lead to deterioration of the psyche, the undermining of an ego that has been steadfastly built with much pain in the hostile world of Hollywood."

This was the reason Dr. Greenson did not wish her to plunge at first, into the unconscious furies of her mind. He hoped that eventually, when she became less the victim of drugs and alcohol, she would be able to look at the terrifying childhood that still ruled her. What the layman Conover did not realize was that if she did not understand the pathetic past, she would slowly become even more tormented.

Somehow she and Arthur Miller, at this time, were trying to make a go of marriage. In Conover's words, "It was not so much a deepening of love and recognition of their common plight. They needed each other. At least it would be the longest time Marilyn ever spent with a husband."

In spite of her unhappiness in the last year with Miller, when *Some Like It Hot* opened to rave reviews in March, 1959, she felt more at ease. Her ego was helped, as Conover pointed out, when she was cho-

sen for the David di Donatello award of the Italian Cultural Institute for her performance in *The Prince and the Showgirl*, the only national award she ever received. As Maurice Zolotow observed, "But
nothing came easily to Marilyn, not her beauty, not her personality,
not her acting."

In early June of 1960, when Conover flew to Los Angeles on business, he telephoned Marilyn to say hello. He thought she would be too
busy to see him but she offered to visit him at once at the Beverly
Wilshire. An hour later she arrived at his door "in a cloud of Chanel
No. 5, her blue eyes sparkling, an ebullient smile on her face." She gave
him a hug and a kiss, said, "It's so good to see you."

She told him at times she called in sick when she really was not ill.
He asked why, she replied, "It's my secret weapon. When I'm late or
don't show up, it costs the studio thousands of dollars. They're always
treating me like a thing. With no brains or rights. How else can I get
a fair deal?"

She also reported her current affair with Yves Montand, said there
was nothing left between Miller and her though they were both heavily committed to their filming of *The Misfits*. She then drew in her breath,
Conover noted, adding, "Meanwhile, I've been terribly lonely. I had
to have somebody—something to hold on to. Yves is very understanding. He's so sweet and kind."

Here she reveals once again that she remained the lonely, forgotten, abandoned-by-both parents child. She constantly sought a
replacement for the first lost man of her life, unable to live alone. She
needed a man's arms around her almost all the time in order to feel
worth while and wanted. This tells us how important it is that a baby,
then a small child, wishes physical comfort from his parents to re-
assure him he is wanted. In her eight years with the Bolenders she
never felt their love, though she could look forward once a week to
her mother's love, as much as she had to give under the painful cir-
cumstances.

Though Marilyn was aware that stealing another woman's husband drew a psychic penalty, for there is bound to be guilt within
such an act, she continued to choose men like Montand who never in-

tended to marry her. Men who would quickly toss her aside, reminding her once again of what she could not bear—abandonment.

After almost six weeks of shooting on *The Misfits* in Reno, Marilyn collapsed from liquor, pills and anger at Miller. Huston shut down the set, arranged for her to fly to Westside Hospital in Los Angeles where she was treated for acute nervous exhaustion. Conover happened to be in the City of Angels at that time visiting his mother, who had suffered a stroke and he arranged to see Marilyn in the hospital.

He recalled, "She was delighted to see me, though she looked pale and weary. I asked her what happened? She said she couldn't stand Arthur anymore. She had to get away from him."

Marilyn started to cry, complained about Miller changing the script and Huston's always wanting to have his own way. She called him arrogant and rude, said, "Women to him are just brainless creatures to be put up with."

As he left the hospital, Conover said he thought, "Out but not okay. Back in Reno she would again have to face the hideous tension of the set, live in daily contact with Miller, and contend with the searing pain of the knowledge that she could not hold on to anyone for long, that in the near future would come the awful process of divorce. Any or all of which could undermine her precarious grip on reality."

She kept hoping, she never gave up on the idea someone out there wanted to marry her. For a time it was Sinatra, whom she saw at intervals. She told Conover when they met in New York, "After one night with Frankie I don't have to see my analyst for weeks." He had given her a gift of emerald earrings.

Marilyn was saying if she felt a man's arms around her she did not need analysis, not understanding the fallacy of this belief, not realizing she was so emotionally disturbed that only by facing her almost unspeakable past could she save her life.

A few months after she moved into her Doheny Drive apartment and was seeing Dr. Greenson regularly, she wrote Conover: "I'm so excited. I think Frankie is going to marry me. He said last night, 'I think we'd make a good team. We're both in show biz, have careers, like to laugh and have lots of fun. Gee, he's sweet. Always so kind and thoughtful. And a real gentleman. I love him dearly. I'll have no sleepless nights with him. Oh, Shutterbug, please wish the best for me." Shutterbug was her loving nickname for Conover, he was, after all, the first "shutterbug" in her life.

Conover wrote in his book he became worried, knowing Sinatra to be too much of a ladies' man and far too wrapped up in himself. "A man of shortlived enthusiasms, his own restless nature was hardly the climate to make Marilyn feel secure and happy in the close atmosphere of marriage," he noted. He called it "a relief and no surprise" when he heard the following month that Sinatra was involved with the dancing actress Julie Prowse, planning to marry her. "I felt sorry for Marilyn," he wrote."Her life seemed to be one rejection after another. No woman ever needed more a reliable and supportive husband."

But a woman cannot expect a reliable and supportive husband unless she is reliable and supportive. Marilyn did not possess this kind of marital strength.

Conover also wrote that he realized no man had understood Marilyn, accepted her, made her feel secure even when married. She had a series of lovers but no one had given a total commitment. Then he added, wisely, "Perhaps nobody could."

The sad truth was that her demands of a man were those of a child on the mother and father. Marilyn needed all of a man's love, attention, sexual activity. She wanted to be the center of his world. This is how a child feels about a parent during the first dependent years of his life. But if the child does not start to trust himself, eventually develop courage within as he seeks his own decisions, he will remain forever the emotionally needy child.

Conover stated that Marilyn told him, "The men I find I'm most attracted to are those least capable of making me happy." If we marry to "make ourselves happy," we are in for a sad jolt. Only we can "make ourselves happy." To depend on someone else for happiness is carrying a strong fantasy from childhood into adulthood, where it does not belong.

Marilyn and Conover met in December, 1961 when they were both in Los Angeles and she was still in her Doheny Drive apartment, near

Sunset Strip. In one month she would be living in her own house she told Conover. She also said she liked her new psychoanalyst very much. Conover wrote,"I didn't like shrinks but I said that he's right about the house. That it would give her a sense of security."

She then said she had to talk to someone, as though apologizing for seeing a psychoanalyst. He noted she seemed in good spirits, looked "really great," wore no make-up, "yet her face glowed from her obvious well-being; her eyes were clear and cool and as blue as mountain skies." He added,"Perhaps this doctor had been good for her, but I hated to see her get hooked to the point where she couldn't function without him."

Conover did not understand that Marilyn had never been able to function alone, without a mother or father substitute by her side she had no confidence in herself. She was still in search of that parent who would take care of her. This desperate need, coupled with a strong urge for the many who would replace the missing "one," meant her life would continue to be meaningless unless she could face the sorrows, the frustrations, the rages of the far past.

She looked sad at one point and Conover said, "Listen, millions of people love you. You're the most adored woman in the world."

She broke into sobs, said, "Yeah, but no man loves me. All they want is a plaything."

Then she apologized, said, "I wasn't being fair. I was only feeling sorry for myself. It's just that I'm in a foul mood. Forgive me." She added, relaxing, "I do need more friends like you, friends who want nothing from me and whom I can trust. It seems like all my friends are people I employ or pay. They all want something from me. Except with the Strasbergs. They've been like father and mother to me. I know they'd never use me or let me down."

He said to her, "You're a very complex subject. Your personality has as many hues as a rainbow."

"You mean I'm complicated?" she asked.

"But in a nice way," he said. "I think I know Norma Jean. But I'm not really sure I know Marilyn Monroe. Because you shift roles constantly, it's difficult to interpret your real feelings. It's as though you can't decide sometimes who you want to be."

"That's my problem," she said. "I'm torn. Sometimes I don't know who I am. It's like hearing voices, each telling you differently what to say and do. Even how to feel. It's terribly frustrating."

She added, "And sometimes I find I have more than two sides, I am so many different persons. I definitely change, with places as well as people. In fact I feel that I'm always in a state of change."

She then asked, "Did you read about the airplane crash? Those eighty people dying needlessly." Conover wrote he could see her shiver. She went on, "It makes me even more conscious of dying. Do you worry about death? I mean, does it bother you sometimes?" He said he did not think of death.

Marilyn was telling him her feeling of self-confidence was very low, her words were of death. She tied together her belief in her self and fear of dying. There were too many early ghosts, too deep a prolonged suffering—as a little girl she must often have felt she would die without a parent substitute.

Her next words were, "I'm afraid of death. But not as much as I am of old age. You should see my arms," and pulled up her sleeves. "Look at these liver spots. They're so ugly."

He reassured her people respected her ability to act but what they most admired was "that in becoming Marilyn, you haven't lost the sweetness of Norma Jean."

She replied, "I can't seem to shake her. Even if I want to. She's my alter ego—very sensitive and easily hurt."

He asked how she was making out living alone. She said frankly, "Not very well. I'm not sure whether I can handle it. But the house helps. It takes up much of my spare time. The worst problem is night. That's when I hate being alone. Maybe I should get married again. What makes the day really worthwhile is having someone to curl up with at night."

Then, as often happened, her mood changed swiftly. She remarked seriously, "Believe me, I don't try to seduce every man I meet. I only like having sex with men I care about. It's more meaningful, not just an animal thing. You really try to satisfy the other person. Besides, it's the nicest way I know to get to sleep. Don't you think so?"

He had agreed but with some reluctance, he said. He described her as being ambitious one moment, an incorrigible romantic the next. He feared that shortly the conflict between these two selves, one a hard-headed realist, the other a wide-eyed believer that anything she wished would come true (again, like a child), would lead to her undoing.

Marilyn kept busy posing for *Vogue, Cosmopolitan* and *Life,* each session consuming hours for tedious makeup and hairstyling. She also flew to New York where the Strasbergs asked her to perform for a few appearances in the role of Blanche Du Bois in *Streetcar Named Desire,* an applicable title for a Marilyn role.

She soon flew back to Hollywood, resumed her sessions with Dr. Greenson. But in spite of the sessions her depression did not appear to recede. If anything, it grew more severe, judging by the alcohol and pills she consumed. She confessed to a friend at times she made up stories because she did not know what to say to Dr. Greenson.

Then a last ray of hope entered Marilyn's heart. She now was courted by a man with whom she fell desperately in love. She expected this brief affair to lead to a marriage that would endure, believed at long last she could change the unhappy sexual pattern of her life.

Most of all, she hoped the new love affair would dispel her wish to commit suicide on the installment plan. A wish that had openly controlled her life perhaps from the day she first became aware she was destined to face one loss after another, no matter how famous she would become or how much money she would earn.

But she was willing to give love and passion one more try. Perhaps this time she would finally discover what she had searched for her entire existence.

**Norma Jean
in high school**
© Robert F. Slatzer

7.
The Final Abandonment

Marilyn first met Robert Kennedy, according to all reports, when she was one of several guests invited to dinner at the Lawford home on February 1, 1962. This elegant beach house, where Marilyn often went to swim in the Pacific Ocean, enjoy a few drinks, have supper with the Lawfords, was the West Coast meeting place for the two brothers, Bob and the President, when they had business to discuss or just wished to enjoy ocean life for a few days.

No doubt Marilyn felt wishes to slip into the ocean nude, as she said she had wished to appear when a little girl in church with her mother. The calendar photograph of her naked before she became famous carried out this wish. So did the many times she appeared nude at her New York home, as Lena Pepitone attested.

At Marilyn's first meeting with Bobby, the Attorney General, and his wife as they passed through Los Angeles at the start of a world tour, she sat at dinner on one side of him as the actress Kim Novak sat on the other side. Later Marilyn asked him questions of a political nature, wanting to know more about the nation's woes.

She next met him on May 19, at her famous "Birthday Salute" to President Kennedy, persuaded by Peter to fly with him in Frank Sinatra's plane to Madison Square Garden in New York, leaving for a few days her appearance in filming *Something's Got to Give*.

As always, Marilyn showed up late. She slowly made her way to the podium, barely able to take a step. She had literally been sewn into an extraordinarily tight, sheer, rhinestone-studded dress. The audience, technicians and television viewers in their homes were stunned to see Marilyn from bosom to ankles appear almost naked, á la Mae West.

Though voluptuous and sinuous, Marilyn also conveyed the "fragile waif" within. The demure part of her, modest and unassuming, flickered in and out of the rhinestone figure. There seemed two personalities—the superstar, Marilyn, and the shy little girl, Norma Jean— who joined each other as they sang in breathless tone "Happy Birthday" to the President.

It appeared as though two separate souls, an often wanton, almost naked thirty-five year old beauty and a quiet, simple schoolgirl, at long last had moulded into one person. There was the innocent Norma Jean and the sexually-charged, seductive Marilyn who enjoyed affairs with "Daddy, the President of the United States." Immediately following her soft-voiced song, President Kennedy said, "Thank you. I can now retire from politics after having had, ah, 'Happy Birthday' sung to me in such a sweet, wholesome way." He received the penultimate birthday gift for lover/daddy over national television.

Following the ceremonies Adlai Stevenson, representative at the United Nations, described how he reached Marilyn "only after breaking through the strong defenses established by Robert Kennedy, who acted like the legendary moth mesmerized by the flame." Arthur Schlesinger, then special assistant at the White House, wrote of Marilyn in his journal, "Bobby and I engaged in mock competition for her; she was most agreeable and pleasant to me."

A few weeks later when the Attorney General flew west for business in Los Angeles, Marilyn and Bobby met again at the Lawford House. According to Paul Moor, who sometimes visited the Greenson home, Joan recalled at this time that Marilyn was excited about "a new man in her life," a prominent person she called "General." Joan thought Marilyn referred to the President until she read in *Life* that Robert was addressed as "Attorney General."

During the months of June and July Marilyn appears to have lived out the most dramatic fantasy of her existence, a drama far beyond any movie she might make. She told her friend, Anne Karger, mother of Fred Karger, her original singing coach, that she was having an affair with Attorney General Robert Kennedy.

The affair was intense but short-lived, within a month and a half Bobby evidently decided, at his brother's request it was rumored, not to abandon his wife Ethel and their eight children, ruin his chance to become the next President, face the threat of ex-communication from the Roman Catholic Church and disgrace the Kennedy name.

Marilyn had told a few friends, including Robert Slatzer, that Bobby had proposed marriage. She now found herself in the denigrating position of once again being ruled out of a man's life after believing he wished to marry her. Bobby would not return her phone calls to his private line in Washington—as her father had refused to speak to her when she called him. This was perhaps Bobby's "unkindest cut of all" though he may not have been aware of how deep a wound he inflicted.

She could not forgive Bobby when he so swiftly changed his plans and rejected her at the instigation of his brother, who also stopped seeing her. The earlier magic of Marilyn's relationship to Bobby turned into bitter rage.

Marilyn evidently told a few friends Bobby had proposed. David Conover's brother, who lived in Los Angeles, wrote David that Marilyn was involved with Bobby Kennedy. Conover decided he had to know the truth, telephoned her. He wrote in his book that she seemed both agitated and depressed, not like her "bubbly self."

She said, "I suppose you know. About Bobby and me?"

He said he did, asked her to tell him everything. She replied, "Bobby said he loved me and asked me to marry him when he got a divorce. Then the bastard ran out on me. I can't get hold of him at the Justice Department or anywhere. He just won't return my calls."

Conover wrote that she sounded hurt, discarded and he suggested Bobby might be busy on government tasks. She also admitted, "I told him I was pregnant." Added, "I had it taken care of right away. It was another tubular pregnancy."

She then said of Bobby she had never known anyone "so two-faced. He could at least have said, 'Thanks. I had a grand time.'"

Gloria Steinem in *Marilyn* says she probably met Jack Kennedy years before his election to the presidency. As early as 1951 the young senator and the starlet attended Hollywood parties given by Charles Feldman, Kennedy's frequent host, at that time Marilyn's agent. Several of Marilyn's friends reported that during the waning months of her marriage to DiMaggio she occasionally saw Kennedy. There were later claims that when the Lawford house was wired by the Mafia, she and the President were taped several times as they lay in bed.

While Marilyn evidently accepted the fact President Kennedy would never marry her, undoubtedly he made this clear, the sudden abandonment by his more sexually conservative brother became to Marilyn a drastic dismissal. It appeared the final insult to her frail psyche. She felt rage deep enough to wish to destroy him but turned the fury on herself—the defense against murdering someone we hate desperately.

One month to the day before she took the fatal step, Marilyn received photographs taken of her by *Vogue*, Earl Wilson reported in his book *The Show Business Nobody Knows*. By then her picture had appeared on the cover of almost every magazine in the world, including "Modern Screen," "Movieland" and "Screen Life." But this was not enough to make up for her defeat at the hands of Bobby.

Weeks earlier, talking about her career to *Life* magazine Marilyn said prophetically, "It might be kind of a relief to be finished. It's sort of like you don't know what kind of a yard dash you're running, but then you're at the finish line and you sort of sigh—you've made it! But you never have, you must start all over again."

She was saying no matter how fast she ran, she could not escape the anguish of the past, forgotten for a moment when she was "running" but then appearing during times of leisure. She no longer wished to start all over again. She had enough of her alcoholic, pill-filled existence.

Two or three weeks before she died Marilyn visited what Anthony

Summers described as "the most dangerous territory of all—the mob-infested Cal-Neva Lodge at Lake Tahoe," reportedly owned by Sinatra and Sam Giancana, the country Mafia boss. There were reports he was also friendly to Marilyn when she visited there. During one night the operator heard "funny sounds" and heavy breathing on the line from Chalet 2, where Marilyn was supposedly asleep, and called the manager, who raised the alarm. Marilyn was saved from another overdose of pills.

The following weekend she "drank a lot," according to Joe Langford who worked under his brother Ray, the Bell Captain. Joe DiMaggio, who felt at home at the Lodge, was still trying to help Marilyn and joined her there. Marilyn later had words with Ralph Roberts, her cherished masseur, confidant and friend, when she returned home, as he recalled, "She told me it was a nightmare, a dreadful weekend. She didn't want to go particularly and when she got there she found Joe. She couldn't go out of her room without the conflict of Sinatra. Joe was terribly jealous of Sinatra."

She now found herself in the denigrating position of once again being ruled out of a man's life after believing he wished to marry her. Bobby refused to return her many phone calls to his private line in Washington, now copying what his father and brother had done, romancing screen queens, becoming "like father, like son."

Five days before her death, on July 30, 1962, Marilyn made her final call to the Justice Department, as shown in telephone records. It lasted eight minutes as she spoke to Bobby, he no doubt warned her he was finished with the liaison.

Her will to live evidently kept eroding, her faith in herself, weak to begin with, slowly evaporated. Perhaps, too, she was starting to face her ever-increasing guilt for trying to steal the husbands of other women. Suicide, as noted previously, has its roots not in one cause but many.

The final affair of her life undoubtedly also reawakened memories of her first abandonment. To a child, abandonment *is* annihilation, one reason Marilyn could never feel worthwhile. Because of the early trauma she acted out her entire life one of her most intense unconscious fantasies. She created the Sex Goddess, the woman no man could ignore or forsake.

Her conscious wish centered on finding a man who would never leave her. But her far stronger unconscious wish, the wish she could not face, the wish that drove her to promiscuity, was to seek a man like her father. A man who *would* leave. Repeating the crime done unto her as a child, she now screamed to the world, "Look what Robert Kennedy has done to me."

Marilyn consciously and unconsciously set up her life so she would abandon or be abandoned, riding on a seesaw of emotions. She left many a man, including her first and second husbands. She either felt exploited by a man or exploited him. We all act out our deepest fears in one way or another, telling the world of our terror, agony and wish to get even with those who hurt us.

A number of signs in the two weeks prior to her death point clearly to her ebbing self-esteem. Following her latest abortion, no matter who the father of the fetus, she would feel exceptionally depressed, like a murderer. She was admitted to Cedars of Lebanon Hospital on July 20, fourteen days before she would take her own life. A death for a death, so to speak.

Self-esteem would also be low because the man with whom she was sexually involved, the probable father of the baby, had informed her he preferred to remain with his wife and children. Marilyn felt no guilt stealing a married man, at least not consciously. Her record included Johnny Hyde, Miller, Montand and now Bobby Kennedy.

Even though she may not have been conscious of seizing other women's husbands Marilyn would feel deep guilt, a guilt that arose from her wish as a little girl to steal her father from her mother. This is the wish every little girl possesses as she prepares emotionally for her later wish to fall in love with a more appropriate male and marry him. With no father on the scene, however, Marilyn would never be able to work through her oedipal desire.

Her affair with Bobby was in a way the match that ignited the guilty, explosive feelings she had so carefully guarded against during the uncertain years as the feelings escalated higher and higher in intensity. They still emerged to some degree in her analytic sessions as she became able to vent the rage of her childhood in the presence of Dr. Greenson, the empathic father and mother figures. He, no doubt, realized she felt as yet too mentally blocked to fully face such dangerous-to-the-ego feelings openly—she might have been driven mad had she started to face them all at once.

Marilyn also copied her mother unconsciously when she sought married men as husbands. Marilyn's father was married at the time he impregnated Gladys so, in a sense, Marilyn followed in her mother's footsteps when she blithely assumed a married man was fair game as her next husband, as with Miller, Montand and Bobby Kennedy.

All the men in her life became in fantasy the cruel father who denied she existed. She sought the love of many to make up in desperate fashion for the lack of the important "one" who had vanished from her life as her mother carried her before birth. Sometimes the man left her first, an act she found intolerable, yet punishment she felt she deserved for being a "bad" girl—wanting daddy all to herself.

Marilyn could not have been true to a man if her life depended on it. She always went in search of the perfect man who did not exist. Whatever her emotional attachment to a man it ended painfully, there was no gracious way out. Norma Jean's love-deprived childhood caused Marilyn to suffer a persecution complex.

❦ ❦ ❦

The final, fatal day of Marilyn's life has been described at length in a number of books. A few have differed as to whether Bobby paid her a visit that afternoon and they fought, whether he was expected that evening at the Lawford dinner party or whether he even showed up in Los Angeles, for he was staying with his wife and four of their children in San Francisco. Eunice Murray, a few years later, said he did appear at Marilyn's house, though up to then she had not admitted this.

Marilyn started to drink early that Saturday afternoon as Pat Newcomb, her friend and publicist at this time, who had slept over Friday night, was present. In the late afternoon Marilyn phoned Dr. Greenson, as she did many a weekend afternoon, told him she felt very depressed. He said he would drive right over.

August 4, 1962 was undoubtedly the loneliest day in Marilyn's exceptionally lonely life. The day before, she had planned a new life, speaking to Jule Styne, producer-composer, in New York. They discussed her possible appearance in a proposed film musical version of *A Tree Grows in Brooklyn*, starring her, Sinatra, Dean Martin and Shirley MacLaine.

She said to Styne, he later reported, "I'll be in New York on Thursday. Can you see me Thursday at 2:30?" He replied, "That's great. See you Thursday."

This was a trip she would never take. She had to endure one month of waiting for Dean Martin to return home so they could continue with *Something's Got to Give*. The one month was too long to bear. She felt too crushed to look forward to happiness in her life, she no longer had the strength even to hope.

In a local call she arranged to meet Sidney Skolsky, the movie columnist and her close friend over the years, to look at new films on Sunday. The Strasbergs were in Los Angeles and she talked to them on the phone about future ventures, trying gamely to keep up her sorrowing spirit.

When Dr. Greenson arrived at 5:15 he asked Pat to leave the house so Marilyn would feel free to talk, sensing she felt disturbed, realized she had been drinking. He would stay two and a half hours trying to calm her down.

He later told a colleague that she had felt "dumped" once more, she had fallen into another "slam bang" affair, far from the true and lasting love she craved. She also expressed considerable dissatisfaction "because she did not have a date that evening." She told him she had expected to see "one of the most important people in her life that night," but the appointment was cancelled. This was obviously Bobby Kennedy.

As he left, Dr. Greenson suggested that Mrs. Murray, who would stay overnight if Marilyn felt upset, take her for a drive along the ocean but Marilyn later told Mrs. Murray she did not want to leave the house.

Peter Lawford called Marilyn about eight-thirty, asked if she were coming for dinner. He had called earlier and she said she did not know what she would do that evening. Now she told him she thought she would stay home. Then in her famous little-girl, soft voice she uttered the warning, "Say goodbye to Pat, say goodbye to Jack and say goodbye to yourself for me. You're really a nice guy."

Before he could reply, she hung up. He was worried, sensing the "goodbye" might be a final one but did not leave his guests to check.

At this time Marilyn told Mrs. Murray, her "caretaker," as she referred to her, possibly remembering the many caretakers her mother had in mental hospitals, that she was going to bed and listen to Sinatra records.

During the evening she received a phone call from Joe DiMaggio, Jr., her stepson, of whom she was very fond. He told her he had broken his engagement, one Marilyn did not approve of. She also made a number of calls, begged Jeanne Carmen, her friend who lived nearby, to come over "with a bag of sleeping pills." Jeanne pleaded other engagements but Marilyn called again, repeating the request. She also phoned Sidney Guilaroff, a prominent Hollywood hairdresser who knew her well, about 9:30, told him, "I'm very depressed," then hung up.

Mrs. Murray later said that before going to bed she noticed a light coming from under the door of Marilyn's room about midnight. She woke at 3:30 A. M., still feeling anxious about Marilyn. She left her bed, crossed the hall to Marilyn's locked door. Then she noticed that the lights in Marilyn's room still streamed under the door and felt alarmed. She knew the pills usually knocked Marilyn out just before she fled consciousness.

Mrs. Murray was afraid to waken Marilyn from her needed sleep, wondered what to do. She felt further alarm as she saw the telephone cord still connected to the inside of the room. After finishing her night calls Marilyn would habitually disconnect the cord so the phone would not wake her early in the morning, treasuring her precious sleep until noon.

Mrs. Murray tried the door to make sure it was locked. She then decided to knock, did so repeatedly but Marilyn did not open the door. Sensing something had gone wrong, Mrs. Murray then walked outside to the front of the house, peered through the locked window of Marilyn's room.

She glimpsed Marilyn lying outstretched on the bed, the lights on as though it were still early evening. Marilyn's hand clutched the telephone receiver which was off the hook, as if preparing to make another call or perhaps just finishing one and not possessing the strength to hang up.

As instructed, if something appeared wrong, Mrs. Murray ran back into the house, seized the telephone and dialed Dr. Greenson's number. He answered promptly, listened to her plea to come over at once, said he would dress and be there within ten minutes.

When he arrived, Dr. Greenson tried the bedroom door, then walked outside to peer through the front, locked window. He went inside, took a poker from the fireplace, walked out to an unbarred window of her room at the side of the house. There he smashed the glass with the poker. He reached inside, turned the handle of the window so he could climb over the low sill.

He stepped into the small bedroom, saw Marilyn, nude, lying face down on the bed. The phone was clutched tightly in her right hand, the phone she had often called her "best friend."

He slowly unlocked the bedroom door, let Mrs. Murray in.

"We've lost her," he said sadly. Psychoanalysts cannot achieve miracles.

He asked Mrs. Murray to call Dr. Hyman Engleberg, Marilyn's internist, tell him to drive to the house at once. He arrived within fifteen minutes, examined Marilyn, agreed "she was hopelessly gone." At 4:25 A. M. Dr. Greenson called the Central Los Angeles police. They transferred the call to the West Los Angeles desk, which covered Marilyn's neighborhood.

When the police arrived, Dr. Greenson told them he thought Marilyn had seemed somewhat depressed when he saw her in the late afternoon, adding, "but I had seen her many, many times in a much worse condition." He said Marilyn had called him as he shaved before going out for dinner and he was glad to hear her sound more cheerful. He told her to get a good night's sleep and phone him in the morning.

The police found on a table by her bed an empty bottle that had contained twenty-five Nembutal pills. A second almost empty bottle stood nearby, its fifty capsules of chloral hydrate had vanished. Other medicines were strewn about the room. Marilyn had used what she believed the saviors of her life but they proved to be the deadly killers.

Before the police arrived, Dr. Greenson reportedly called Peter Lawford, who raced to the house and destroyed all evidence of letters written by Bobby, then left swiftly. Marilyn's notebook, describing her feelings about Bobby, also disappeared.

Summers was given access in 1984 to talk to Dr. Robert Litman, one of two Suicide Prevention Team members, psychiatrists of the Los Angeles Suicide Prevention Center. Dr. Litman had studied under Dr. Greenson, respected him greatly, and "felt it right not to talk about this until after Dr. Greenson's death." He had died five years before on November 24, 1979 at the age of sixty-eight.

Referring to early 1962, Litman wrote: "Around this time, Marilyn started to date some very important men...at the highest level." Dr. Litman also reported that Dr. Greenson spoke of a "close relationship with extremely important men in government," saying the relationship was "sexual."

Dr. Greenson added he was concerned because Marilyn had been "used" in these relationships. He did not take a stand against these romances, he said, because they seemed to gratify Marilyn's need to be associated with powerful and important men. But he cautioned her, he added, to be sure she engaged in the relationships because she thought them valuable to her, not because she was "driven" to do so.

Whether Marilyn killed herself purposefully or "accidentally on purpose," as the saying goes, by swallowing fifty or more Nembutal and chloral hydrate pills, does not matter. "Purposefully" is a conscious act, "accidentally on purpose" an act caused by an unconscious wish to end one's life. One might say Marilyn was on the one hand user and abuser but on the other, the innocent victim.

Marilyn did not die from the classic combination of alcohol and pills, though drugs were the key. Tests showed 13 milligrams percent pentobarbital in her liver and 8 milligrams percent chloral hydrate in the blood. Pentobarbital was the chemical identified in the sleeping pill. Nembutal and chloral hydrate were two of the less dangerous sedatives found in Marilyn's home.

Her Nembutal intake was found to be ten times the normal therapeutic dose. The chloral hydrate level alone indicated a "fairly stunning intake," up to twenty times the amount usually recommended for sleep. Either of the drugs, taken in such quantities, could individually have proven fatal, according to Summers. Taken together, they were even more likely to kill.

ಕ ಕ ಕ

When Marilyn died Dr. Greenson received letters from psychoanalysts all over the country sending their condolences, saying how difficult it must have been for him to try to help a tortured Marilyn. He had waged a valiant but losing fight to prevent her suicide.

She had prepared well to destroy a life she could no longer cope with. The men at the top did not want her, where else could she go? What new fantasy could she use to make life worth living? In her mind the alternatives were either madness or death by pills. Her mother and grandmother chose madness when their men deserted them. Marilyn chose pills, to her the preferred way to exit from her excruciating emotional pain.

Marilyn used the last evening of her life to cut off her mortality. Even the immortality she had gained over the years was not enough to make up for that final abandonment which cut to the heart of the original one. She had affairs with the two most powerful men in the country—the President, knowing he would never marry her, and his brother, the Attorney General, who promised to marry her, then broke his promise. This for her was the end of the line of irresponsible lovers. She dared risk no more.

One psychoanalyst wrote Dr. Greenson, "In the case of Marilyn Monroe I think that having no mother around when she grew up, no father, no brother, no sister, created a severe identity defect. When such men and women become promiscuous they do so because the act of sex gives them a sense of identity.

"At the moment of sexual fulfillment they feel themselves. It is this fear of not knowing oneself, this fear of not *being* oneself, which also drives to drug abuse. On a 'trip' one feels oneself and for people of this kind that is the highest fulfillment."

He explained further, "Many actors and actresses suffer such a defect as they accept assigned identities, play their roles effectively. Even some of the greatest actors confess they are always acting, even when not filming. They can do this because they do not have that kind of strong ego normal people do. This makes the actors more vulnerable to mental illness."

He concluded, "Marilyn in a sense never knew who she was. The change of name a movie star often undergoes makes him feel he is two or more personalities and his tortured life may end in disaster. This is shown by the numbers of actors and actresses who commit suicide or die early from alcoholism or drugs or overdose on sleeping pills."

The roots of suicide stem not from one or two causes but many, as pointed out previously. Marilyn's final affair with Bobby Kennedy made her feel deserted, reawakened her mother and father's abandonment. Because of her parents' desertion, she acted out in her adult life many of her most intense unconscious fantasies centering on Norma Jean's loneliness, her belief she was alone in the world and would always be, no matter how many psychoanalysts she saw.

No single person can be blamed for Marilyn's death. She showed clearly after she became a success and started to drink heavily and swallow endless pills that she was headed for suicide. The Greenson family was grief-stricken. Dr. Greenson said he was sure it had been an accident.

Who was there for Marilyn to depend on during her whole life? "Do you know who I've always depended on?" she once asked W. J Weatherby, noted journalist, who covered the 1960 shooting of *The*

Misfits for the *Manchester Guardian*. "Not strangers, not friends. The telephone! That's my best friend. I love calling friends, especially late at night when I can't sleep. I have this dream we all get up and go out to a drugstore."

This is a dream straight out of childhood, a dream of the days when, as a little girl, her happiest memory may have been eating ice cream on Saturdays with her mother at a drug store. It is childish thoughtlessness to call friends when they relish needed sleep just because her own momentary panic drives her to this outlet.

But finally the telephone had failed her, too, it was no longer enough solace to call a friend late at night. She tried early in the evening that fatal Saturday, could not find anyone to comfort her. The last comfort, the only comfort that remained, were the pills.

All her life she had only herself as rescuer if she wanted to survive. She was successful the first thirty-five years. But then she succumbed to emotional wounds so deep she could no longer be her own rescuer. The lovely, adorable, sexy goddess would never again have to worry about "going crazy." Or being abandoned. Or sleeping alone at night, no warm arms embracing her.

The strong defenses she erected as a fortress to save her sanity finally crumbled as she doomed herself to death by her own hand, consumed by a rage she could not endure. She died still mired in the misery of her early past. Misery she could no longer bear after adding to it all the guilt along the way from childhood to stardom.

She could never kill others, not even the man at the top who jilted her. Her only alternative had been to turn the murderous feelings on herself and end her tormented journey, suffer her last abandonment.

I asked Paul Moor if he thought Dr. Greenson had made a mistake, as some psychoanalysts believed, in allowing Marilyn to become virtually a member of his family. Paul said, "I asked Romi this same question. He told me, 'Absolutely not. She has never been included in a warm, harmonious, loving family and that was the therapy she needed more than anything else in the world. Not only I but my family wanted to help her.'"

When Marilyn died Dr. Greenson felt very depressed, according to someone close to him who explained, "It's difficult to lose a patient any time, but above all, somebody you care about. Also a patient who is in the limelight. Dr. Greenson had to work through a loss, a mourning period."

Marilyn believed sex was her salvation but it proved part of her doom. We all mature in our own timing, some faster than others, some perhaps never if not helped to understand the past but take to drugs and drink, as Marilyn did. They need to live in a "phantom world," as Dr. Joseph Sandler, the prominent British psychoanalyst, described it, out of a need to cling "to the internal objects we have constructed during our development—our 'ghost objects.' They provide a source of reassurance against the painful aspects of life. They bring two worlds together, the fantasy world and reality as we externalize objects of our outer world."

Marilyn's inner world held terror and rage, her outer world for the most part encouraged her to seek the heights in films and sexual activities. She could go no higher than the President of the United States and his brother, the Attorney General, but at least the partial conquest of both for a certain period of time would attest to her ability to possess sexually the most important, glamorous men in the country.

Marilyn mourned all her life, the need to mourn was ever-present and vital to her existence. If this need is slighted during analysis, if the patient continues holding within his depressed feelings, if he does not allow himself to cry, scream, show abject misery at the loss of loved ones with whom he is deeply identified, who have become part of him—one of the "ghost voices" within that is now both his conscience and his terror and at times target of his own hatred—he will not have been successfully analyzed.

The emotion of mourning, the loss, had to be felt deeply within Marilyn as she shed tears in Dr. Greenson's office, bewailed her fate. He took a chance, a great gamble. He knew she had spent four years of analysis with a highly reputable woman analyst during which Marilyn must have felt some relief from the demons pursuing her in dreams. She was intelligent, willing to explore her mind and feelings further. What could she lose? If he failed to help her, he would be the one accused of the loss.

Dr. Greenson was aware of Marilyn's pain and blocked-off rage but he also saw courage, for it is courage that brings the unhappy to the couch. Many fear to tackle awareness of the inner mind because of the emotions that tore Marilyn apart. Her rage at her father, her unrecognized, overpowering need to mourn her mother, forever absent in mental hospitals, her wish to kill those who had hurt her, her strong, uncontrollable sexual needs.

Her achievements in seeking men brought her right to the top and when they dumped her, where could she go, after reaching the heights? It was then her fury became uncontrollable. Some authors of books about her life said she threatened to make public Bobby Kennedy's affair with her, furious when, after proposing to her, he realized to marry her would destroy his chances of becoming the next President. It was said this was in the diary Peter Lawford took from her bedroom as he raced over in the dead of night.

Perhaps, too, part of her suicide was awareness of her wish to destroy Bobby, feeling she would if she remained alive. Then deep hatred of self emerged and she could not resolve the dilemma—kill herself or kill Bobby's career by revealing to the world their affair. She chose to destroy herself, swallowing a deadly amount of pills.

Many of us are afraid to tackle the awareness of unconscious, buried feelings and wishes because they stir emotions believed "bad" and "wicked." Dr. Greenson took the gamble that Marilyn would be able to give up the harmful liquor and pills and thus free herself to speak of the deeper emotions.

In spite of all he could do to try to help her face her inner self, for Marilyn the pain ended soon and precipitously. Within that inner self still dwelled the baby, the child, the girl and finally the beauty the world knew. But there also surged the relentless Norma Jean.

In essence, Norma Jean murdered Marilyn Monroe with the devastating memories even Dr. Greenson could not reach. They had been buried too long and too deeply and the strong defenses Marilyn erected against allowing them to break free would not fall. Not even with

Dr. Greenson's sympathetic help and his family's loving intercession.

Her pain in early life ran too deep. There was a long-time murderous feeling within Marilyn, as in all of us to some degree and she was about to turn it on herself in full fury as she stuffed an unbearable amount of sleeping pills down her throat the night of August 4, that sorrowful Saturday in 1962.

Dr. Greenson later admitted to a colleague after her death, "I had become a prisoner of a form of treatment that I thought was correct for her but almost impossible for me. At times I felt I shouldn't go on with this." There were days he saw her three or four hours either at her home or in his office. He knew she was too emotionally distraught for formal analysis as yet but he was willing to risk that becoming part of his family might bring Marilyn enough comfort so she could become a true analytic patient.

I asked a well-known psychoanalyst who lived in Los Angeles but did not want his name used, his opinion of Marilyn's illness. He told me, "Her need for love was a bottomless void. It could never be filled. When an infant is so severely traumatized in the first years of her life, nothing can be done. This a therapist has to accept. Some therapists, especially when they grow old, think they can do everything and will try to help anyhow. This leads to tragedy for patient and therapist. The therapists actually sacrifice themselves in order to fill that void. It may have even contributed to Dr. Greenson's early death."

This psychoanalyst also emphasized that Marilyn never really felt beautiful because "only a person who feels loved feels beautiful. Men liked her fragility. That activates all the rescue fantasies of men. It is more attractive than a beautiful body. These are the women who try to seduce their therapists not through desire but their own needs."

He says that his own diagnosis "would have been 'hospitalization,' a word which Dr. René Spitz, the well-known psychoanalyst, coined." He concluded, "Severe traumatization in infancy cannot be analyzed. It needs a corrective, emotional therapeutic experience which a therapist cannot give to the extent needed. So many symbols in this poor girl's life meant death. Sex, for instance, meant death, not sexual fulfillment. As the French say, 'Le Petit Mort.'"

At the end Marilyn turned all fury on herself—suicide is the wish to murder inflicted on the self. Suicide is also a serial killing—the wished-for death of those many persons who have deeply hurt the victim. Looking at Marilyn's life from the day she was born, what she achieved in thirty-six years was awesome. She had conquered the world in one area but there was no way she could make peace with the subtle early terrors of her life.

Psychoanalysis is never easy for the patient. Many devastating parts of the self require a long time to understand and accept. Tears flow, anger rages as slowly, very slowly, the hurts and wishes of the past become part of the conscious mind. There are failures in psychoanalysis because childhood, as in Marilyn's case, was too horrendous for the patient to accept.

Marilyn's mother and grandmother chose madness when their men deserted them. Marilyn chose pills, to her the preferred way to exit from her excruciating emotional pain.

ಠ ಠ ಠ

The mystery of why Marilyn was so afraid to live alone in her house can be explained by the fact that the first real family home she knew, at the age of eight when she moved in with her mother, she was forced to leave after three months as her mother was taken to a mental hospital where she would remain most of the rest of her life.

When Marilyn, twenty-eight years later, finally owned her own home near Dr. Greenson and his family, she lived in it six months, twice as long as she had lived with her mother, then gave up, preferred death to losing her mind.

What strength Marilyn mustered throughout her career went into playing roles onscreen and keeping face and body beautiful. The moment it seemed as if she might never be offered another film, she ruled out any chance to discover the suffering self within that would have kept her alive. When Robert Kennedy unceremoniously dumped her, as though saying, "You're not good enough to be my wife," this was exactly what her father had contemptuously tossed at her mother when pregnant with Marilyn, dooming her mother and herself to a lifetime of loneliness and despair.

Norma Jean might want a lasting love of marriage and a child but Marilyn felt this as detrimental to her star role—nothing must be allowed to stand in the way of her importance as actress. Thus the many abortions.

Marilyn won the battle in that she was loved, accepted, praised by most of the world for her singing and acting. But she lost the war when she was unable to look within herself and understand why she had felt so tormented all her life.

She did, however, at times possess a strong sense of humor that drew men and women to her. Much humor emanates from our need for laughter to ameliorate life's harshness. Humor is often a strong defense. Marilyn was "emotionally fixed" about three or four years of age, a time little girls are most seductive to the masculine personality. She impressed the Bolenders as a very cheerful child, a behavior that often masks depression.

"Just as a person's fever is guide to the health of his body's functioning, the thermometer of a person's emotional functioning may depend on the use of alcohol and drugs as barbiturates," points out Dr. Alma Bond, prominent psychoanalyst, author of *Who Killed Virginia Woolf?*

Dr. Bond explains, "Dr. Greenson tried to persuade Marilyn to cut down on her pills, but she could not, by that time they had become her most driving necessity so she could sleep at night, dominating the unevenness of the struggle to survive. The forces that kept her alive for thirty-six years were no longer powerful enough to fight her wish to die.

"Marilyn as a child felt worse than if her mother had forsaken her outright, not even seeing her once a week. To Norma Jean, each day her mother was not there (which occurred at least six times a week, sometimes seven) and each time her mother left her it was like pulling a scab off a deep wound.

"It kept her in a perpetual state of mourning, unable to form new lasting attachments—men or women—always feeling they would forsake her. I think her problem was basically with her mother who proved psychotic and could not give her daughter constant mothering. So she was never able to develop what we call 'object constancy,' where the child is able to keep an internal image of 'the good parent.'"

Dr. Bond believes that "even though Marilyn spent five years with two of the world's finest psychoanalysts—Dr. Marianne Kris and Dr. Ralph Greenson—it wasn't enough to undo the damage. Her mother lacked a solid love she could not give her daughter. As a result, Marilyn raged all her life at the mother who rejected her. The few months her mother spent with her in her apartment, as Marilyn tried to get her own career underway, did not work out and her mother soon was carried back to the mental hospital.

"When a child does not have a mother she often looks to the father figure to rescue her. But Marilyn's father had deserted her the moment he knew Gladys was pregnant. Repetition of her father's rejection which, combined with what we could call almost total loss of her mother the day Norma Jean was born, led to her eventual suicide. It is highly unlikely that any analyst could have helped Marilyn recover her sense of worthiness unless the awareness of her fury and helplessness started in the analyst's office when Marilyn was in her early teens."

Marilyn also had "this appealing quality many mentally disturbed men and women often possess which makes others reach out to try to mother them." This was clearly apparent in the years she lived with Arthur Miller.

Marilyn's use of humor as a defense was not strong enough to carry her beyond her thirty-sixth year of life. Where could she head after she felt four years with Dr. Kris had not helped her understand herself, nor did the year with Dr. Greenson?

Her constant use of drugs and liquor had turned her slowly into a Zombie. She knew what that meant—the mental hospital. Consciously or unconsciously, by overdosing she told the world she could not tolerate this indignity. She preferred to take her own life.

Norma Jean as a model
© Robert F. Slatzer

8.
The Triumph
Of Norma Jean

Marilyn was a gambler—you have to be if you contemplate the road to success in Hollywood. The odds against you run high but if you succeed, the payoff is equally high.

She started to realize, with the help of Lee Strasberg, who urged her to go into analysis with Dr. Kris, that fame alone would not ease the emotional pain within. She had to find out why she could not sleep, drank to excess, took pills that would knock her out of reality so she could sink into a night's rest.

The fact she sought Dr. Kris's help, then Dr. Greenson's, shows at long last she wished to understand why she was slowly destroying herself with booze and barbiturates.

The odds were against Marilyn, not the Hollywood odds she conquered, but the odds of being at heart the emotionally damaged Norma Jean, who would no longer allow Marilyn the star to continue to pretend she could sail through life without paying dearly for the ongoing destruction of mind and body.

Marilyn's early life and early death is the story of Beauty (Marilyn's feelings of pride as a star, her career veneer, so to speak) and the Beast (Norma Jean's feelings of fury at her unwanted, demeaned self as a child).

These two parts were in constant conflict as, in a sense, they are in each of us but not to such an extreme. We have one picture of ourselves as a successful adult, another as an angry child when we felt enraged at parents for not understanding us, not loving us enough. The beast lies in all of us—our sexual and aggressive wishes have to be tamed. When they are not, to a reasonable degree, we see the rapist, the seducer of children, the murderer and the tortured soul who commits suicide.

Not Marilyn's fame as film star or her glory as sex goddess on and off the screen were enough to keep her alive. Stardom and success did not count because they were up against a dark, vicious enemy, the self within Marilyn that slowly formed from the day of her birth.

"I can't imagine buying a house alone," she said, when she moved in, "but why can't I? I have always been alone." Thus she described her entire life.

Her last abortion occurred on July 20 in Cedars of Lebanon Hospital, there for four days as she had "surgical termination of pregnancy." Zanuck is alleged to have told her she would lose her shape after having children and she made sure this would not happen. She damaged her inner body to such an extent that when she wanted to have a child after marriage to Miller, she could not.

Marilyn was not only idolized when alive but lives on as no other screen star has. She would have been sixty-six on June 1, 1992.

Forbes magazine on October 3, 1988 listed ten "dead artists whose names still make money for those to whom the artists left their wealth." Marilyn's name was eighth on the list. Elvis Presley was first, followed by Ian Fleming, John Lennon, Jimi Hendrix, T.S. Eliot, James Dean and Jim Morrison.

Announcement appeared in *The New York Post* on December 4, 1989 along with a photograph of Marilyn, her eyes closed, her lips pursed for a kiss and the words, "Marvelous Marilyn: Sex goddess at the height of her career."

It was accompanied by a story announcing that the four-poster, handcarved English oak bed she shared with DiMaggio during their nine-month marriage in 1954 would be auctioned off at the Regal Antique in Ho-Ho-Kus, New Jersey. The minimum bid was set at $25,000.

On Monday, December 18, 1989 Cindy Adams' column in the *Post* carried the news the 141-year old double bed was bought by Japan's Mitsui company, which owns the Highpoint Woodworking Company in High Point, North Carolina, for $60,300, more than double the minimum bid. The bed's original owner, Cindy revealed, was Nathaniel Hawthorne. Mitsui's chairman said he was shipping the bed to an antique oak furniture museum in Tokyo. Marilyn will have new glory there.

At Sotheby's in New York on December 15, 1989, a dazzling sequined floor-length dress Marilyn wore in *Gentlemen Prefer Blondes* reached a bid of $14,300 but was pulled from the block because this was not the $20,000 minimum set by Sotheby.

Eddie Jaffe puts into words his feeling about Marilyn starting with her first important screen appearance in *The Asphalt Jungle* in 1950. He says, "As one accustomed to trying to understand my own feelings, first I thought of her body language and how her face seemed to say, as well as the words she used when she called Louis Calhern 'daddy,' 'I need a father.'

"I also thought of the camera as having a romance with her.

"Part of what I felt was professional for it was my business to try to understand what an actress had to offer a film maker, how the public would feel about her. I said to those who would listen to me, 'that blonde'—I wasn't even aware of her name—'is going to be a most important star.'

"What also impressed me, a quality I regarded as important for an actress was that she did not censor her emotions. She was willing to let you know how deeply she felt, whether it was her longing or her sexuality. As a press agent, I recognized she loved attention, loved publicity, put no barriers against it no matter how physically threatening as the crowds closed in on her, tried to touch her."

Jaffe says that even after she became one of the most famous personalities of our time, sought by famous men, part of her "always remained the girl from the days during the war when she worked in an airplane factory. The audience could sense this and identify with her both then and now."

He believes part of the answer as to why her memory is so strong among so many, may be that "she never fell out of love with her audiences, her fans. She needed their love and they sensed and appreciated this." He adds that those who ask for autographs are in essence asking, "Loan me a part of your fame, this is more important than giving me money, having your name on a piece of paper. She knew how they felt and was happy to loan her fame to anyone who asked, to make their life more bearable as they were making hers."

He believes that what has contributed to her becoming legend and a myth, in part, will endure for centuries, that the audiences sense she was asking the question, "Who am I?"

Did the women in the audience sense she had contemplated suicide, recognized the terror underneath the provocative smile? Jaffe says, "I am sure that in every film, the four-year old Norma Jean was very much present," an astute observation no one else has made. The child Norma Jean was, in Marilyn's feelings and wishes, a large part of the reason she was late on the set, drank so heavily, was driven to pills, had to be sexually involved with a man or she did not feel alive. We can never divorce our earliest years from the rest of our lives.

There was a paradox in Marilyn's inner life in that she would pose nude for a few hundred dollars because she needed the money, Jaffe points out, but she refused to accept millions from men, including Johnny Hyde, who wanted to mention her in his will, knowing he was dying, and Joseph Schenck,who asked her to marry him, saying she would inherit sixty million dollars when he died.

Sam Shaw, noted photographer and movie producer, worked with and befriended Marilyn in the mid-1950s. He had been hired by Charles Feldman in 1955 to shoot a set of publicity stills to promote her in *The Seven Year Itch*. Twenty-four years later Shaw published these and other photographs in *The Joy of Marilyn in the Camera Eye*. He has produced photo essays on many film directors and movie stars, also served as executive producer on the majority of films directed by John Cassavetes.

Shaw describes Marilyn in the book as "joyful, playful in high spirits, in love and out of love. A ripe Rubenesque beauty bursting with the sensuous fun of living, at work and in moments of reflection. I call this assemblage of photos 'The Joy of Marilyn.' She created that comic-tragic figure we all know and too often she didn't know herself from the creation. This got worse as time went on, when she became the victim of her own fantasies and illusions. But the Marilyn I remember most is the woman of joy and fun I show in my collection of photographs."

Shaw adds, "After seeing these photos, one is deeply saddened to see her as she really was and by such an untimely end. But, as she said in the title of the caricature she did of herself—'What the Hell—That's Life.'"

When Marilyn married Miller, Shaw gave her a set of books on the artist Goya from the Pardo Museum in Spain. He also took her to the Metropolitan Museum of Art where the etchings of Goya were on exhibition. She stopped before a Goya Black Horror scene of witches flying through the sky at night, monsters on parade.

She grasped Shaw's arm, said, pointing to one monster, "I know this man very well—these are my dreams." Man to her was a monster, her father was the original "monster" in her life.

Shaw says Norman Rosten introduced her to poetry and was understanding and compassionate, never made demands on her. He and his wife were close friends of Miller's, he collaborated on Miller's script for the play *View From the Bridge*.

When Shaw went to the Miller home in Connecticut to do a *Look* story with Jack Hamilton on the newlyweds, Marilyn asked him, "Sam, what do you think of the quartets?" He did not know what she meant by "the quartets" until later in the day when he realized she spoke of Beethoven's quartets. He thought she meant the Modern Jazz Quartet. He had taken her, before her marriage, to see and hear Nat King Cole, knowing she was interested in jazz but Miller introduced her to the world of Mozart, Beethoven and the theater, all of which she took very seriously, Shaw says.

At the same time she was an avid reader of fan magazines, "most of all her favorite reading was her fan mail. There was a period when her fan mail was loaded with vituperative hate. She showed me some vicious cranks that put her in a terrible depression."

She was not, to him, "a Calendar girl, although Tom Kelly's *Playboy* nude shot was the greatest calendar type photo. She was a contemporary Aphrodite who could transform into Hogarth's Shrimp Girl, Franz Hal's lusty bawdy tavern peasant beauty, in off-guarded moments a reflective Saskia or Rubens' 'graces,' especially her back view. Sometimes a pensive child—with thumb in her mouth."

Shaw says her idols and goddesses were Jean Harlow, Betty Grable and Jane Russell, "not only for their beauty—she thought Harlow the most beautiful ever—but for their personal life and struggle which she seemed to know in depth. I never explored or asked her to explain."

He also describes her as "making her own fashions, ahead of her time. Twenty, thirty-five-years ago she was like the young women of today. She was the first to wear jeans. She would get a new pair of jeans, go to Santa Monica beach, walk into the sea, drenching the jeans until they clung to her body, then stay in the sun. The jeans dried to her form and fit her like a well-worn glove."

He describes one day in Manhattan when she was in her bedroom making up for *The Seven Year Itch*. Half dressed, she calmly applied her makeup by the light of a tiny 20-watt bulb. The amber glow of light forced her to accent her eyebrows, lashes, eye shadow, lipstick.

He said to her, "That makeup is outrageous, so exaggerated," he did not say it was vulgar but implied this. He noticed that DiMaggio, then her husband, "a stickler for time, obligations and the right thing" had been "graciously holding his exasperation in," though he felt the same way as Shaw did, "he loved her but, a reserved man, he preferred the girl beneath the famous camouflage."

Marilyn looked at Shaw and said, "This makeup is for my fans, my public, those people who are waiting in the crowd across the street. They are the people theaters make pay to get in. When I come to the theatre I'll turn to them and wave and they'll see me and won't be disappointed." Added, "*They* want me glamorous."

She needed to feel glamorous, that the world loved her, because in childhood she felt no one did. But now even the telephone, the instrument on which she had always depended when she felt low self-esteem finally failed her when she could not reach those she called that last night of her life.

While living in New York, Marilyn had wanted to know more about politics, mixed with men and women who would talk freely in this area. She went to lunch one day at Sardi's with Lester Markel, Sunday editor of *The New York Times* for nearly half a century. He then gave her a guided tour of the newsroom. After his death in the seventies at the age of eighty-four, his daughter Helen discovered, stuffed in the back of a desk drawer, a letter Markel had received from Marilyn in March, 1960. She wrote:

> Lester dear,
>
> Here I am still in bed. I've been lying here thinking—even of you...About our political conversation the other day: I take it back that there isn't *anybody*. What about Rockefeller? First of all he is a Republican...and secondly, and most interesting, he's more liberal than many of the Democrats. Maybe he could be developed?...Of course Stevenson might have made it if he had been able to talk to people instead of professors...Ideally, Justice William Douglas would be the best President, but he has been divorced so he couldn't make it.

She concluded the letter saying she hoped to see him soon again when she would wear her "Somali leopard," adding, "I want you to think of me as a predatory animal." She signed the letter, "Love and kisses, Marilyn."

At one point Strasberg had approached Marilyn to play Sadie Thompson in *Rain* on television. He later said, "I thought she could do that quite superbly. She had a kind of colorfulness, a strange romantic quality, mainly this gauzelike quality, this tremulousness, together with other things she had that didn't need to be worked for."

Unlike the married minister in *Rain*, who converted the prostitute into a Godlike young woman who refused his love, whereupon he killed himself, though Marilyn might blame Bobby, she alone was responsible for her death. It was caused by what she felt the ongoing misery of her life.

If someone refused to love her, to talk to her, it was similar to hate, just hearing another voice represented love and caring. When there was the connection, even over thousands of miles, to someone important in her life, whether make-up artist, producer or Attorney General, there was important verbal contact. Something she missed almost completely as a child. It was as though these later calls were an attempt to make up for the early non-existent ones.

Norma Jean was born innocent, we are all born innocent. Like Narcissus looking into the water she must have asked, "When do reflections stop and reality appears? What is the real part that lies within me?" She also had to ask herself, "Why have I wished not to have a family?"

🐞 🐞 🐞

The burning question, as Sean O'Casey, the poet, posed it seemed to be, "Who killed Marilyn Monroe?—That was a tragedy."

Norma Jean killed her. Slowly but surely. The little girl who grew up to become the glamor queen of the world. Norma Jean lay buried within, though at times escaping, as Marilyn confessed, biding her time, accepting the pain until she could no longer bear it.

Who was it that walked into Dr. Greenson's office? At times it was Marilyn, at times, Norma Jean, the ripples between the two occurred many an analytic hour. Somehow the last abortion proved the final straw, how many times can a woman abort? The damage done by abortions can be devastating to the soul. The two times she desired a child, living with Miller, she failed to deliver a whole one.

Marilyn finally became tired of being the abandoned child crying out, "Someone love me, please love me," to every man with whom she had sex. Following which she left him or forced him to leave her because of her outrageous demands that he be the good parent of childhood she never possessed.

The last years of her life the signs of self-destruction rang clear as a bell tolling her doom. They signalled in anguished detail the presence of a fragile, failing inner self. She made it clear she had been emotionally programed from the day of birth to take her life at an early age, at the time she felt most desperate, most unwanted and most shattered within.

Guiles wrote Marilyn "was dedicated to *survival*. To making it through the day and especially through the night. There was something at the core of her being that felt absolutely, terrifyingly alone—a place in her that seemed immune to human support and reassurance."

What was this destructive "something" at the core of her being? What horrors haunted her, killed her will to live? Only Norma Jean knew and Dr. Greenson was trying to make it possible for Marilyn to know too, if she could give up the alcohol and drugs used to blot out the miserable past. But she was unable to achieve this in time, the pain of daily existence was too powerful, outweighed her wish to understand herself.

At times, she said, it felt as though she possessed a number of personalities. She once remarked to Lena Pepitone, "I would like so much to have one personality. You could say any one person is many people and Norma Jean is still alive inside me but in quite a different way. The Norma Jean I remember was the poor, always-hungry kid of the foster homes and the orphanage and later the one who would hang around in the agents' office every day, hopelessly waiting for a job."

Then she added, "There's something in me—a third person maybe—which makes decisions for me, and they're final. Another of my personalities keeps them under wraps and plays on as if nothing had happened. But it *has* happened. And I'm such a coward that I continue to act as if I didn't know what's already been decided."

Perhaps when she mentioned she was a coward, pretended not to know "what's already been decided," she referred to her impending death. That Norma Jean had made the decision there would be no more play-acting, no further pretense that life was worth living if this last attempt to return to Hollywood, again a divorced woman, failed to bring her happiness.

She spoke of the "vital lie" she often played in front of others "until I can't go through with it and can't sleep and take too many pills and break down and have to begin from the beginning again...I never get out of my own vicious circle." This is quite a confession she makes in referring to her "vicious circle."

Then she mentioned the deepest fear of all: "I think about my mother, locked up in a mental hospital, and that my grandmother and grandfather died insane and I'm on the verge myself."

Her promiscuity would add to her guilt, a guilt that was constantly with her. One psychoanalyst explained, "Promiscuity has many causes. In the case of Marilyn Monroe I think that having no mother or father around when she grew up created what we call a severe identity defect.

"When such men and women become promiscuous they do so because the act of sex gives them a momentary sense of identity. At the moment of sexual fulfillment they feel themselves. It is this fear of knowing oneself, this fear of not *being* oneself, which also drives to drug abuse. On a 'trip' one feels oneself and for people of this kind that is the highest fulfillment."

He concludes that Marilyn "in a sense never knew who she was. The change of name a movie star often undergoes makes him feel he is two or more personalities and his tortured life may end in disaster. This is shown by the numbers of actors and actresses who commit suicide or die early from alcoholism or drugs or overdose on sleeping pills."

Dr. Greenson knew Marilyn sought love and devotion without conditions, that anything less was unbearable. This was, of course, an impossible demand for anyone to fulfill—another fantasy of fantasies.

Marilyn had been deprived of going through the natural oedipal stage because she lacked a father to love passionately, as most little girls do when they start on the road leading to the love of a man they eventually marry. Marilyn remained unconsciously pinned to the lit-tle-girl wish to sleep with daddy, unable to mature beyond it, emo-tionally speaking.

Whatever her emotional attachment to a man it ended painfully, there was no gracious way out. Norma Jean's love-deprived child-hood caused Marilyn to suffer a persecution complex she would never lose.

ೆ ೆ ೆ

Dr. Greenson faced Marilyn in her dual roles as both patient and friend of his family. She was somehow a special patient in dire need of help. She took offense at the slightest irritation on his part, she de-tested the notion of imperfection in "certain ideal figures in her life, she could not rest until peace had been reestablished," he wrote a colleague.

When she first started analysis he saw her six, perhaps even seven days a week at times, mainly because, as he later wrote, "she was lonely and had no one to see her, and nothing to do if I didn't see her." He had become her whole world, as is apt to happen at the start of psy-choanalysis.

He said she revealed two clear "problem areas": her obses-sive fear of homosexuality and her inability to cope with any sort of hurt. The fear of homosexuality in a woman shows her wish to be loved by another woman and to love another woman. This is a normal feeling usually outgrown at three or four years of age when the little girl turns to the male parent for love. But there had been no one to whom Marilyn could turn from birth on for steady love and guidance.

Dr. Greenson wrote of Marilyn, "She couldn't bear the slightest hint of anything homosexual. She had an outright phobia of homo-sexuality, and yet unwillingly fell into situations which had homo-sexual coloring, which she then recognized and projected on to the other, who then became her enemy."

It may have been that Dr. Greenson did not realize that for Marilyn to live in a house by herself, which he persuaded her to do in February, 1962, might have reminded her of the house her mother rented in which Marilyn for the first time lived with Gladys. From then on, unconsciously "house" to Marilyn may have meant a step closer to being carted off to a mental hospital, as her mother was—a kind of death she wished to avoid more than anything else in life.

She was not strong enough to learn through adversity, the way most of us survive. Many do not learn from adversity, they complain, blame others, feel sorry for themselves, as Marilyn did. She had the right to do so because of the cruelty of parents unable to love her.

Dr. Greenson died of heart failure at the age of sixty-eight, seventeen years after the death of his most famous patient. According to Dr. Robert J. Stoller, who wrote the obituary for the *International Journal of Psycho-Analysis* in 1980, this meant the loss of one of the profession's "most glowing, articulate and creative clinicians."

Dr. Stoller wrote of Dr. Greenson that "everyone was his teacher...there was a quiet place within that let him listen well. There lay his art...he heard better than the rest: about the working alliance and the real relationships; about empathy, boredom, identification, transference, depression, enthusiasm; about technique as the source of true insight and the fundament of analytic research.

"In the solitude of our practice, where we all are students it is too easy to hear nothing but the sound of our own theories, a grand narcissism that corrupts good sense. Greenson had none of that at the core.

"He knew—and so much enjoyed knowing it—that the central feature of psychoanalysis is the relationship between patient and analyst. From that awareness, that organic commitment, came his therapeutic brilliance, innovative techniques, contributions to analytic theory, and his unparalleled clinical descriptions. Therein he was, precisely, an artist...he also was blessed with the capacity to transmit his data to us by means of his words. He wrote to reveal, not hide, clinical reality and his explorations were powered by intense and compassionate empathy, not by dogma and disquisition. The record of his life shows that he knew how to search and where to find, and then respecting the value of what he found, he could easily share."

Dr. Stoller also pointed out that anyone could sense the power of Dr. Greenson's "love" in the many papers and books he published, cited "especially his great *The Technique and Practice of Psychoanalysis*." Dr. Stoller said Dr. Greenson "could only think and write by pouring himself out, searching for the sources of mental life in the living, sentient experience...only from that bountiful though mysterious well did he then—later, carefully, with roots in the realities of the quickened analytic treatment—turn to theory."

Dr. Stoller described Dr. Greenson as "the greatest of teachers." He referred to "the writings, first because they shall keep speaking to us, keep asking their questions and serving as models for how we might search for the answers that can only be found in psychoanalysis... He lectured to medical students. He taught innumerable analytic seminars. He rose out of his seat at meetings and shook the architecture of psychoanalysis..."

Dr. Greenson was in the top echelon of the *International Psycho-analytic Association*, his work respected all over the world. One of his most famous papers appeared in the International's Journal when he reviewed "The Writings of Anna Freud," Volume IV, a collection of papers written during a period in psychoanalysis when important new developments and divergences were becoming increasingly apparent in the psychoanalytic movement. The title of Dr. Greenson's review was "The Voice of the Intellect Is a Soft One," one of Freud's sayings—"The voice of the intellect is a soft one, but it does not rest till it has gained a hearing."

In an article Dr. Greenson said he believed Freud's statements in reference to the difficulty in ridding oneself of illusions "are remarkably apt in describing the writings of Anna Freud." He pointed out that she began by setting forth some of the major controversial issues. She believed the child's family cannot be excluded from the analysis. Their "good sense must take over most of the role of the adult patient's healthy ego, his motivation for treatment, and his therapeutic alliance... the little child's inability to use speech makes child play therapy very different from psychoanalysis with adults." Dr. Greenson pointed out that child analysis should only be undertaken when speech was more fully developed.

"In evaluating the child's infantile neurosis it is important to realize that the child's suffering is equally divided between the child and the parent," he said. "Much of the child's anxiety may be bound by phobic or obsessive symptom formation and the amount of suffering will be determined by the reactions of the environment."

Dr. Greenson praised Anna Freud for her papers on "feeding," in which she pointed out that "if eating becomes invested with great aggressive and sexual meaning, it can lead to depressions, melancholia and anorexia nervosa...Food and mother remain linked forever in the child's unconscious...Most of the child's conflicts about food are transferred from the mother."

Possibly no one mourned Marilyn as deeply as Dr. Greenson did. As Hildi Greenson described her husband's treatment of Marilyn, "Basically, Romi had to be very optimistic vis-a-vis his patients. I don't think a therapist could function otherwise, albeit he must possess a touch of skepticism. As far as Marilyn being a part-time member of the family, I thought it was a worthwhile attempt by Romi to ameliorate her terrible loneliness. Lacking even surrogate parents and being shifted to, I think, at least six foster homes, would certainly be a very desolate start in life, particularly given her own poor genetic background."

In her marriage to Miller Marilyn had to face her failure as a woman, as a mother, as an adult. But she was a top star, she would achieve even higher praise for her role in *The Misfits* as the young woman who made the plea to save the wild horses as Marilyn had made personal pleas to save fish, dogs, any living animal that seemed threatened by man.

She also had the powerful fantasy she wished to be a man. All little girls, at one point, wish they had been born a boy, believe boys are "treated better, loved more" and also boast that extra bodily possession that creates a baby, the phallus. Part of Marilyn wanted to be masculine, strong, not a weak, impoverished, deserted, whimpering little girl.

To survive as a child Marilyn no doubt fantasied herself at times as both man and woman, mother and father to herself. She was doomed never to feel fully feminine because a part of her wanted to be the strong man, the one in charge. Who "loves 'em and leaves 'em."

🍎 🍎 🍎

We learn from Marilyn's tragic life that if we do not face and understand the frightened, tormented child in ourselves we will never feel whole and happy. As Freud once said, "To be completely honest with oneself is the best effort a human being can make."

The life of a celebrity holds a special pitfall. The average person exults when the mighty and the successful "fall from grace." This reassures the more plebian person the celebrity is less well off than he is, that money and success do not bring lasting happiness. That if there is such a thing as happiness, the less successful can find it more easily than the celebrity.

The task lies within us all to give up—which means accept consciously—much of the distorted fantasy world of the child so we may know and deal with as graciously as we can the limitations of reality. Marilyn could not achieve this. She dwelled too deeply in her make-believe world because of the acute pain of her early days. She was unable to cope with, much less face, the later demands of reality. She remained an uncertain, breathless, seductive, tormented little girl, frightened to death at the idea of growing old.

She often sought men and women who would take advantage of her as, in her way, she took advantage of them. She was unable to give mature love, feel tender toward, truly care about another human being. To know mature love you have to feel the touch of love as you grow up. Or, as Dr. Greenson was trying to help her realize, know you did not receive enough love from a parent, accept this and stop blaming both the parent and the self.

Marilyn's seductive voice, her lovely face, her sequined, low-cut, body-clinging dresses could not erase the earlier torment as the desire for revenge on those who once hurt Norma Jean slowly took over the glamorous, shimmering, artificial world Marilyn Monroe created for herself.

Eventually she suffered more than she could bear because her search to find her "true self," as psychoanalysts call it, was too blocked by her need to take on a "fictitious" or "false self." The self-created sex goddess of the world no longer was a match for the abandoned, screaming Norma Jean.

Marilyn's success in the world of filmdom was accompanied by slow death at her own hands. In the fight between her two selves, the true self and the false self, the former had to understand the latter and the latter, the former, so both could survive. But the fictitious self of filmdom did not have the strength to conquer the overwhelming pressure of the true self of childhood, partly at times an angry, quietly screaming one.

Marilyn's "real self" had been wounded too deeply too soon in life. The "false" self, the self so successful in exuding sexual desire in films and in her personal life ad infinitum, tried to provide a lasting panacea. But the anger of Norma Jean, the torn-apart, unloved little girl, finally triumphed as killer of both the false self and the weakened real self.

Men and women attracted to the acting profession, according to psychoanalysts, feel comfortable about playing the parts of imaginary persons but often possess little sense of their own identity, perhaps one reason they choose the profession. It is difficult for many of them to adjust to life's disappointments and frustrations as the ordinary mortal is expected to do That is why we hear of so many broken marriages, illicit love affairs, breakdowns, suicides, even occasional murders among actors.

Marilyn lived in a "no-win" situation. She could never give up the childhood terror of going insane, ingrained early as a child by seeing her grandmother, then her mother, taken to a mental institution. One of her fantasies probably blamed her father's walking out on her mother without marrying her as the cause of her mother's insanity. This fantasy may have pervaded Marilyn's mind each time she felt abandoned by a man.

The Hollywood scene could only foster her fear and fury, as well as her sexual desire, her one way of gaining assurance, though an ephemeral one. At least she felt temporarily loved, better than no love at all. She learned early that ambitious starlets were expected to have sex with producers, directors, famous actors, columnists and anyone else who could help them along the way to success.

If something within—Norma Jean, perhaps—objected to this promiscuity, Marilyn dared not show it, she had learned early to repress fear and anger and would continue to do so. As a little girl she rarely cried, had revealed a warm, generous nature, though she did tell her mother when the Bolenders punished or severely struck her.

Marilyn recalled seeing her mother occasionally weep for no apparent reason or laugh hysterically. A woman who remained mute for the most part when her daughter visited her in mental hospitals. We can only guess at the depth of Gladys' fear and fury, with a father, then a mother who both sank into madness.

It appears as if Norma Jean started to take over slowly, but with lasting vengeance, following Marilyn's disastrous marriage to a former member of the nation's championship baseball team. DiMaggio wanted his own way, wished his new wife would give up films, see him as the man in her life. Marilyn remained four and a half years with Miller but even the help of a psychoanalyst could not sustain the shaky marital relationship, compete with his attachment to his muse, his writing. It was all she could do to keep herself on a steady keel, what with the stream of alcohol and pills that now plunged into her body.

But she was determined to make one last try to face the truth of her distorted life as she bravely sought Dr. Greenson. He tried to help her understand she could not rely on some "magical" lover to miraculously end her misery.

Aware of her addiction to sleeping pills and alcohol, he tried to help her take the first step of giving up the dangerous barbituates. Her final purchase of a vast number of pills was a defiant act against his wishes, as though saying, Even you cannot help, my life is too tormenting, I have no hope the future will be any happier

Thus Norma Jean slowly triumphed over Marilyn Monroe as

the latter's attempt to understand her misery crumbled. Without sex to lull her to sleep, she remained awake and in misery. Without the phone she was forced to face all the fearful fantasies of her life that swarmed into consciousness, as they are apt to do in the middle of the night. It is then the unconscious part of our mind tries to break through and give partial release to our strong sexual and aggressive desires.

Marilyn's lust for sex was not only fueled by her strong adult sensual desire but by a longing from childhood to be held in her mother's arms, where sexual feelings start. Her search for a mother was clearly seen in her emotional dependency on the two women who became very close to her, one at the start of her career, the other at the very end.

Both were her acting coaches, first Natasha Lytess in Hollywood and later Paula Strasberg in New York who seemed to see in Marilyn a key to the power she sought after years of living in her husband's shadow. Each woman, one at the start, the other at the end of Marilyn's career, was present on the set (much to the anguish of directors) telling Marilyn how to act, giving her emotional support. This revealed her deep dependence on a woman, a childlike trait she could never give up.

She had built her fame on her provocative little-girl walk and voice. Come-hither eyes. Perfect breasts and body. Lovely face. Also a quick sense of humor. In spite of her extremely cruel childhood, she somehow mustered the strength to use humor in both acting and her personal life when not too distraught.

But in the long run Marilyn's humor was not strong enough to defeat her desire to vanish from the earth because she could no longer stand what she believed her unloved self. She had remained emotionally a child, which meant she still believed the world revolved around her, as children do. A child thinks his every wish should be fulfilled, he cannot accept frustration without feeling fury.

Three days before her death, in an interview that appeared in the August 3rd issue of *Life*, Marilyn said, discussing herself, "You're always running into people's unconscious." But it was *her* unconscious—

the buried feelings, fantasies and wishes of Norma Jean, the deprived, angry little girl—that killed the glamour queen of filmdom.

One of those fantasies centered on the loss of Bobby Kennedy. This had triggered Marilyn's belief she could no longer attract a man. If she lost her ability to be the sex goddess of the world and became a shriveled up, middle-aged woman, she felt she had two choices— madness or death by her own hand.

Her early, intense feeling that life was not fair, she was not like children who lived with parents as she grew up, drove her to the final decision. She openly set the scenario of her death, piling up so many pills she had to know there would be no return from oblivion once she started to take them. Ironically, she died almost thirty-five years to the day her grandmother had been committed to the Norwalk State Hospital, there to die nineteen days later.

At last Marilyn had become consumed by a rage she could not handle. It was either murder—of the man who had just jilted her—or suicide. She could not kill anyone else, the only alternative was to destroy herself.

The abandoned Norma Jean finally took revenge on the cruel world into which she was born. That Marilyn Monroe lived as long as she did, trying valiantly to overcome the inner fear that haunted every step of her famous climb to fame, is testimony to her great courage.

The death of Marilyn Monroe was Norma Jean's revenge on the two people who brought her into this world, then fled, left her to fend for herself as best she could.

Marilyn's modest home bore a stone inscription in Latin over the front door. Translated it read, "My Journey Is Over."

Her exciting but terrorizing journey through life had ended. Now she could sleep forever, untortured by the punitive past.

🐛 🐛 🐛

One of Marilyn's most moving songs was titled "Bye Bye Baby," from *Gentlemen Prefer Blondes*, a memorable song and a memorable performance of seduction and wistfulness. In her death, Marilyn was saying "Bye Bye Baby" to Norma Jean.

Dr. Greenson told a colleague after Marilyn's death that the Miller marriage had collapsed "to a considerable degree on sexual grounds." Marilyn believed she was frigid, he said, and "found it difficult to sustain a series of orgasms with the same individual." He added, "This thirty-six-year-old woman still thought of herself as a fragile waif."

This was no fantasy, she *had* grown up as a fragile waif, she told the world this in her films—her life was a genuine plea for pity and for love.

Her screams in the final scenes of *The Misfits* at the men about to murder wild horses and sell their bodies, were Marilyn's screams to the world that insensitive cruel men were out to kill *her*. She identified with the horses as she did in reality with the fish and the birds. Miller was then divorcing her, Montand had thrown her over, their brief affair ended. Miller's film even dressed Marilyn in a white dress printed with cherries, the "cherry" meaning a virgin in blue-collar jargon.

Susan Strasberg spoke of the day she lent Marilyn her sketch pad and pen and Marilyn completed two drawings. One depicted "a feline sensual grace and movement," as she did a self-portrait. The second "was of a little Negro girl in a sad-looking dress, one sock falling down about her ankles," Susan explained, added, "I thought that was a self-portrait, too, of Marilyn's hidden self." Portrait of Norma Jean, the bereft, black little orphan.

One day Susan told her, "Marilyn, I wish I were like you."

Whereupon Marilyn gasped, "in that sometimes whispery voice and said, 'Oh, no, Susie. I wish I were like you. I'd love to have your family. People respect you.'" Susan commented of this moment in Marilyn's life, "She trembled with the intensity of her feelings."

Marilyn's love for Paula was evident. One Christmas the doorbell of the Strasberg home rang, Susan's parents opened the door to find no one there. A wrinkled brown paper bag lay on the doormat. Paula picked it up, peered into the bag, drew out a leather jewelry case. It contained a single strand of pearls held by a diamond clasp. Marilyn had given Paula the necklace the Emperor of Japan bestowed on her during her honeymoon with DiMaggio. Marilyn knew Paula loved pearls.

Susan wrote that with Marilyn's death, she felt ashamed and guilty because she had "resented the attention Marilyn had attracted from my parents. Her need was greater than mine. I longed, but she demanded: Help me, feed me, love me, love me. And they had, protecting her as long as they could, except in the times when their closeness threatened her in some way and she would withdraw."

Susan believed that "perhaps for Marilyn the demands of the film world and the real world had finally become equally painful, so that there was nowhere to escape." She added, "But she had been so alive. An iron butterfly, some people had called her. Butterflies are very beautiful, give great pleasure, and have very short life spans." She added, "It was strange, I couldn't imagine Marilyn as old. Her childlike quality seemed to defy the demands of time."

That childlike quality emanating from Norma Jean was one cause of her death, the early fantasy that life was one long party, offering fun and frolic.

In his eulogy, delivered at the Village Church in Westwood, Lee Strasberg said, "We, gathered here today, knew only Marilyn, a warm human being, impulsive and shy, sensitive and in fear of rejection yet ever avid for life and reaching out for fulfillment...she was a member of our family."

A loving two-page article about Marilyn by Clifford Odets appeared in *Show* magazine, October, 1962 three months after her death. She had a part in Odet's film *Clash By Night* ten years before, playing a fish cannery worker. The article was titled "To Whom It May Concern: Marilyn Monroe," with the subtitle "A Prominent American Playwright's Requiem for a Tragic Golden Girl."

His first paragraph read, "One night some short weeks ago, for the first time in her not always happy life, Marilyn Monroe's soul sat down alone to a quiet supper from which it did not rise. We cannot know her last words or thoughts, but it is likely they echoed Yeat's remark, 'Life seems to me a long preparation for something that never happens.'"

He spoke of Marilyn having an "invisible dark companion," who whispered, "Abandon, before you are abandoned, again yourself!" Odets then asked, "Or was it that what Marilyn craved most was an adequate parent, not merely a husband?" Odets knew her greatest need.

❦ ❦ ❦

We learn from Marilyn's tragic life that if we do not face and understand the frightened, tormented child within, we will never feel whole and happy. Norma Jean early learned to survive on fantasies, one of which was seeing herself as a famous movie star. Her greatest conscious fantasy was the creation of Marilyn Monroe. But the persistent fly-in-the-ointment for her emotional wounds was that Norma Jean always seethed underneath her new persona, would always seethe just below the surface of her glamour and fame.

Norman Mailer wrote in his 1973 book, *Marilyn,* that he believed she was "in the deepest need of a cure." He said, "Her illness is made up of all that oncoming accumulations of ills she has postponed from the past, all that sexual congress with men she has not loved and all those unfinished hours with men she has loved, all the lies she has told, all the lies told about her, all unavenged humiliations sleeping like unfed scorpions in the unsettled flesh. Worse!-all unfinished family insanity, plus her own abused nerves. Plus the need to come to rest in some final identity."

Dr. Herbert S. Strean, a leading psychoanalyst mentioned earlier, was asked if he believed we ever forgive parents for their cruelties, real and imagined. He replied, "It's a matter of degree. The more we can forgive, the mentally healthier we become. We have to accept what our parents did to us without hating them for it, knowing they had parents who treated them in the same way. They too felt hurt as children. As adults we have to judge them also by the many things they did to help us, as well as hurt us. And to realize no one can be the perfect parent. This is an unreal, not a real demand."

The word "narcissism" has often been used in connection with Marilyn. Every child is narcissistic, believes the world should bow to his needs, tell him how wonderful he is. As Freud said in his first work on narcissism, *Leonardo da Vinci, A Study in Psychosexuality*, "In general it is no longer possible to doubt the importance precisely of the first years of our childhood. "

Psychoanalysts have made major contributions that bear out his assertion. They found, for instance, the origins of depression and delusional fantasies appear in the first few months, if not days, of our life, long before we have learned to think rationally.

Psychoanalysts also stress the importance of the roles of "aggression" (hate) and "libido" (sexual drives) in the formation of our mind. They point out that the way such feelings are felt by an infant in the early exchanges with his mother will determine whether he becomes a very angry child or a happy, peaceful one. Failures in such exchanges, whatever the cause, set up emotional roadblocks on the road to maturity.

As a result of battles and frustrations that may arise between child and mother, the child may hide anger, find no outlet for his rage and automatically turn it back on the self. The child senses early in life that to display anger against the person who takes care of him is far more dangerous to his survival than to try to forget what he considers an insult and smile grimly. If our caretaker casts us out who is there to feed us, love us?

Research has shown that the infant, during the first year of life in particular, is happier the less frustration he feels. A mother can never be too gratifying, she must be prepared constantly to meet her child's need to be soothed, comforted, held, spoken to, sung to. At the same time she should protect him from the anxiety and impatience all mothers feel at times. Ideally, she should hold back all angry feelings, regardless of the frustration the infant's crying may evoke.

Aggression turned on the self applied in spades to Norma Jean, who had her mother only once a week. Norma Jean had to make sure she never offended her mother or her own life would be in danger.

❦ ❦ ❦

Marilyn's death was an international shock, unexpected throughout the world. The day her death was proclaimed many a man and woman gasped, "I don't believe it! Why would she want to kill herself?" Her millions of admirers had no inkling of the misery in the life of the star Montand described as "the most tortured woman on earth. She lived in a hell."

Marilyn embarked on the toughest road to fame and for thirty-six tormented years bore her overwhelming inner burden. Her sense of humor onscreen and off, her valiant fight to become someone "important" who "mattered" to other human beings as she survived by her own wits, were herculean in the face of her early psychological wounds. It took additional strength for her to carry out her wish toward the end of her short life to know what had gone wrong as she sought the help of two psychoanalysts.

Marilyn wept convulsively, she recalled, the first time Zanuck gave her a contract, as though she did not deserve such luck. For her to be noticed, rewarded, approved of, loved, stirred guilt, followed by tears. Women often cry over something they feel guilty about, men hold back the tears but feel guilt too.

Marilyn had too many tough battles to wage. The fight against her illegitimacy. The fear as a child caused by feeling alone in the world. The desperate wish to be loved and wanted in strange foster homes as the uninvited guest of unwilling hosts. The battle against insomnia as inner guards fought against nightmares that expressed her terror. And last, but not least, the fight against drugs that placed her in an oblivion that blotted out all memories of the injustices of her life.

Marilyn never knew who she really—and unreally (in fantasy)—was. Her name was not her own when she entered the kingdom of the stars as Norma Jean receded more and more to her mental underworld, the protector of easily wounded feelings. Marilyn fought hard to preserve her sense of sanity which all her life she dreaded would one day be taken from her.

Almost twenty-eight years and four months after her death a television program titled "Marilyn: Something's Got to Give" was shown on December 13, 1990 at 9 P. M. on Channel 5 in New York City. The program proved a documentary of the last months of Marilyn's life as she appeared on the set of the doomed bedroom comedy, with the same title as the television program. Photos taken on the set and dialogue never heard before, long buried in a Kansas warehouse, were shown for one hour.

The audience saw a Marilyn breathtaking in her beauty, far slimmer than ever, her face exceptionally happy as she was filmed with the two children who were part of the cast. The narrator said of Marilyn, "She had a beauty and a sexual glow no one ever could touch." She had lost fifteen pounds before the start of this film, he said, and resembled "a Goddess."

The plot involved her sudden appearance after five years of being supposedly lost at sea, at the home of her newly-wed husband, played by Dean Martin, his wife, played by Cyd Charisse and Marilyn's two children who did not remember their mother.

She spoke in her soft voice with its undertone of humor, her laugh-clown-laugh mask, as though the world were one large joke. Her final movie, a comedy, which would never be completed by Twentieth Century-Fox, was the last picture she owed them. The one-hour television program was the result of six hours of unedited scenes strung together as raw fragments of the whole.

The filming had started on April 10, 1962. She would be thirty-six on June 1. Harry Weinstein, producer of the film, who spoke on the television show, said of Marilyn, "She didn't have to perform, just look good." He added that she was "mentally fragile at times" and arrived "hours, even days late" on the set, psychologically unable "to get anywhere on time." He knew she took barbiturates, he said, because one day he saw her at her home acting "mentally unstable" from pills .

Fox was teetering in losses produced by the film *Cleopatra*, starring Elizabeth Taylor and Richard Burton, which had cost $30,000,000 to produce. Feeling in a precarious economic position, the studio had shut down everything but Marilyn's film, desperate for a hit, as the narrator explained. She was paid $100,000, one tenth of Elizabeth's fee.

Marilyn started to call in sick on April 30, explaining she suffered a sore throat and fever of 101 degrees. The film, incidentally, was a remake of the 1939 *My Favorite Wife* which had starred Gary Grant in a similar plot.

The one-hour television film concentrated primarily on pho-tographing Marilyn as she talked to her two children beside the pool of the house where they lived. She appeared "emotionally tender to them," in the narrator's words. As though she wanted to care for them the way she wished she had been cared for as a child.

Joan Greenson Aebi, who kept Marilyn company as she walked outside the Greenson house until her hour started, appeared briefly as part of the program. She described Marilyn in the film as "tender and very consoling," added, "her poise made her beautiful."

Marilyn possessed that rare quality of conveying her feelings, be they sexual, sorrowful or comic with such earnestness that the viewer empathized with her. Whether in the depths of despair or flirting with a man, there was no pretense. Her heart was in her work, in these moments her anguish vanished.

The narrator of the hour-long television film said, describing Marilyn in what would be an attempt to appear in her unfinished, final movie, that she was "looking like a different Marilyn, her face was thinner, more assured, tender expression in those lovely blue eyes. She spoke her lines with a feeling of love for the children." The children she had never been able to produce.

George Cukor, director of the ill-fated film, known for his patience and gentle manner with stars, particularly Marilyn, said she would "throw up" at times before a scene. She would also ask worriedly, "Was I all right?" showing as little confidence in herself as the very first time she appeared in a picture, he said.

She suffered from insomnia and exhaustion and by May 19th had missed fifteen of the first seventeen days of that month on the set. "Is she here?" the cast would ask every morning. Would she show up at all, was the question, followed by, "Was she up to making a movie?" She had one doctor for her sinusitis, another for her eyes, an internist for her organs and her psychoanalyst for her mind.

But it was not always her fault. A delay of many fifteen-second se-quences with the dog Tippy, took a whole day to film as Tippy kept blowing his cue. One scene showed her laughing as she held Tippy close to her and remarked, "I used to come here a long time ago, he remembers me." These words were part of the film's plot but one wondered if Marilyn had named him "Tippy" after the little dog she loved when a child at the Bolenders, who had been shot by a neighbor for invading his plants.

Then occurred the famous pool scene at midnight as she mischievously slid out of the flesh-colored bathing suit and dogpaddled nude. Meanwhile the audience saw Dean Martin inside the mansion, filmed as breaking the news to his second wife that his first wife had miraculously returned home. Then the strains of the song "Something's Got to Give" sounded and the camera showed Marilyn climbing naked out of the pool—the first nude scene by a major star, according to the narrator.

Unfortunately, the four hours she spent photographed in the pool aggravated her virus and once again she phoned in sick. Dr. Engelberg, her internist, was as always willing to supply her with prescriptions for sleeping pills, going against Dr. Greenson's wish that she give them up.

Marilyn continued to remain close friends with Dean Martin, her ally, who appeared undisturbed by her lateness or her days away from the set. He was patient and understanding, the narrator said, and "when she was late, he would stand swinging his golf club."

She was fired temporarily when she left to sing "Happy Birthday" to President Kennedy in New York but six weeks later rehired at twice her salary, according to the narrator. Meanwhile Dean had made arrangements to appear in nightclubs during the summer but agreed to resume work on the film in September when his tour ended.

Marilyn could not wait. A few weeks later she was dead.

❦ ❦ ❦

A well-known Hollywood psychoanalyst summed it up: "To Marilyn, death by her own hand was preferable to killing another person or going mad. It was not merely the loss of Bobby, but what that loss meant to her in terms of her childhood fantasies. Our childhood fantasies are our most powerful fantasies because they are created when we are most impressionable. Hopefully, later we acquire the courage to face them so they no longer drive us to compulsive, destructive acts.

"Marilyn tried to use sex as a soporific and painkiller. It worked for the moment but failed to remove the pervading inner demons. Throughout her career she turned her anger, not deliberately but unconsciously, on a number of prominent directors by appearing late for shooting, holding up production, forgetting her lines, all of which required numerous retakes. In her fantasy the director represented the father who had refused to admit she was his daughter. *Though he was totally absent in her life, he was ever-present in her unconscious.*"

The director also stood for the foster father who struck her when she disobeyed, with whom she lived the first eight years of her life. "In the fight between her two selves, Norma Jean and Marilyn, one had to die, making it impossible for the other to survive. The 'true' or 'real' self never had a chance because the Sex Goddess had no confidence in either self. If Marilyn felt downed by any hurt in life she could rarely show it (except, finally, after four years of marriage, toward Arthur Miller). She early learned in the foster home to repress rage or suffer violent beatings by her 'pretend' father. She was taught, as most children are, not to strike back when an adult hurt her but repress her fury. Eventually the rage in Norma Jean, the torn-apart, unloved little girl, finally triumphed as murderer of her thwarted, hated self. Marilyn sought too late the facing of that hated self, which is the aim of psychoanalysis."

The psychoanalyst concluded: "Dr. Greenson tried to help but it was too late. The battle against him proved too devastating. Sleeplessness, sex, drug abuse are all death equivalents. Addiction or no addiction, it was relatively unimportant in Marilyn's case. The only important thing was her self-destructive drive. All her life part of her wanted to die, from beginning to end. People with a strong drive to die are deeply afraid of dying. This is the reason Marilyn could not sleep, sleep is the twin brother to death, death is called 'the big sleep.'

"Marilyn was afraid to die and therefore afraid to sleep. It is this duplicity that for lay people is difficult to understand. The message of

Marilyn's life is that a person can possess opposing wishes. Her sleep-lessness was caused by the fear of going 'insane' and losing control of herself when asleep, then dying."

This psychoanalyst concludes, "Marilyn was a sex kitten, an or-phan, always pleading to be loved, offering herself as an immature, almost virgin-like lost soul. In later life she desperately wanted a child of her own to love. She must have instinctively known the love of a child would make her feel loved and in this way teach her how to love, but all her attempts to carry a pregnancy failed. She never truly loved one soul in her short stay on earth.

"In essence, she was sexless, a murderer (of herself) and insane (living partially in a world of fiction, not reality)."

❦ ❦ ❦

Marilyn sought help too late. A psychoanalyst cannot perform mir-acles if the emotional damage runs deep. The psychoanalyst can only attempt to help, hope he can somehow ease the patient's pain. Noth-ing Marilyn could achieve of fame or fortune could fill the bottomless well of her loneliness or lack of faith in herself. All the sex in the world could not make up for the fear in her heart that no one could possi-bly love her, nor she, them. Robert Kennedy was the last of many to prove this, he made her feel unwanted, assailed within mind and body.

Hollywood has been accused of "killing" Marilyn, making her life more difficult even as she made the film company richer. But Marilyn unconsciously arranged for her own death—not because Hollywood refused to pay her enough or give her more dramatic roles but because of the many unhappy episodes in her early life. Marilyn's burdens in-cluded her traumatic childhood, which led to her inability to express true and lasting love for anyone, man, woman or child.

Marilyn wrote in an unfinished autobiography, "I knew I belonged to the public and to the world, not because I was talented or even beau-tiful but because I had never belonged to anything or anyone else." This is a tragic statement.

In her last film appearance, *The Misfits*, Clark Gable speaks lines that are pure Miller, as they applied to Marilyn's life: "Sometimes when a person doesn't know what to do, the best thing is to stand still." But she could not, at this point in her tortured life, muster the emotional strength to become that mature.

The enveloping fear of killing a man for leaving her—she could leave many but no man could desert her—slowly took over Marilyn's thoughts, culminating in the triumph of Norma Jean. The death of Marilyn Monroe was Norma Jean's revenge on all the men and women who had hurt her during her life but primarily the man and woman whose sexual liaison created her, then left her to fend for herself in a cruel, uncaring world, devoid of love, affection and constancy.

In Miller's film Marilyn asks questions directly out of her personal misery, captured by Miller, as well as out of the fictional young woman she portrays. When Gable tells her to "just live," she asks, "How do you 'just live'?"

She may have been aware this would be her final film, she lacked the inner substance to appear in any more but also sensed that not appearing in a film would destroy her.

Gable says to her at one point (Miller's question to Marilyn), "You're a real beautiful woman but what makes you so sad?" Then adds, "You're the saddest girl I ever met."

Miller portrays the rivers of torture running through Marilyn's mind that revealed her underlying panic which she unconsciously at times brought to the surface from her very heart.

In one scene she says in desperation to Gable (Miller's words), "Love me! Love me!"

In another scene Gable, drunk, totters into the ramshackle house in which they temporarily live as lovers. Marilyn remains outside the door, looks up at the sky, whispers, "Help!" How many times this plea to the Lord must have occurred to her in real life.

Still another moving scene occurs toward the end of the film, after the men tie up the horses they intend to sell to those who will kill the stalwart animals, make glue out of their bodies. On seeing this cruelty, Marilyn races out into the desert, screams, "Murderers! Liars! I hate you!"

Here she reveals how she feels toward the men in her life who lack feelings for those not strong enough to fight back. She protests the barbarism of men who inflict death on innocent animals. But she is also screaming her hatred of the men she believes deceived and deserted her, Miller included.

The final scene pictures Gable and Marilyn driving away in the blackness of night from Reno, hoping their newfound love will last.

Suddenly Marilyn asks in her soft, seductive voice, "How do you find your way back in the dark?"

She was never able to find the way.

PN 2287 .M69 F73 1992x

Freeman, Lucy.

Why Norma Jean killed
  Marilyn Monroe

WITHDRAWN

STATE LIBRARY OF OHIO
SEO Regional Library
Caldwell, Ohio 43724